Starting with abstract painting

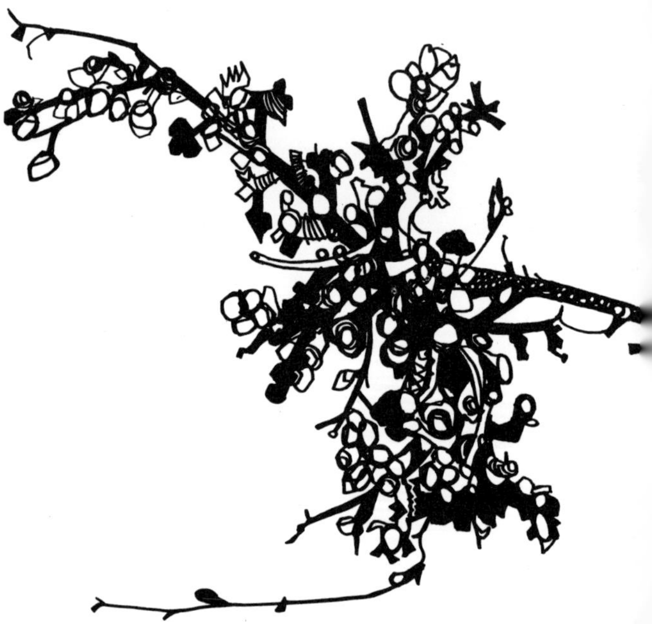

Starting with abstract painting

and abstract work in other media

Kenneth Jameson

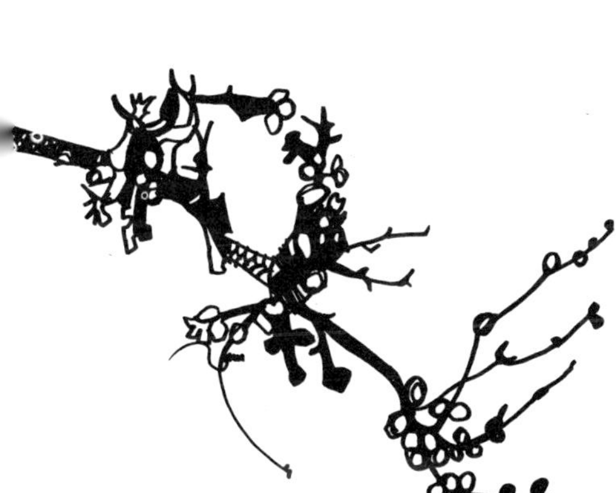

Studio Vista London
Watson-Guptill Publications New York

Acknowledgements

For the illustrations in this book I have drawn upon photographs, reproductions and original works from many sources. I would like to acknowledge help in this respect to the following:

The Amalgamated Playing Card Co. Ltd for fig. 109
Mr Phil Brodatz for the use of two photographs, figs 37 and 43, from his book *Textures* (Dover Publications Inc., New York)
Students of Coloma College, West Wickham, Kent for figs 34, 35, 36, 48, 60, 61, 114
Croft Radio Ltd for permission to photograph their window display, fig. 142
Ivon Hitchens CBE for fig. 13
Johnathan Masters for fig. 62
Midland Bank Ltd for allowing me to use the photograph in fig. 140
John Nash for fig. 11
The Paul Nash Trust for fig. 12
Ben Nicholson for fig. 141
Miss Heather Padfield for fig. 49
William Scott for fig. 8
The Trustees of the Tate Gallery, London for permission to reproduce figs 2, 7, 8, 10, 11, 12, 13, 14, 83, 96, 141
Mrs Muriel Whittaker for the two photo-micrographs, figs 93 and 94
In addition I would like to thank my wife, friends, students and pupils for their co-operation

'Pied Beauty' by Gerard Manley Hopkins, page 6, is published by permission of the Oxford University Press on behalf of the Society of Jesus as owners of the copyright

The cover design is a section of a cauliflower stalk

General Editors Brenda Herbert and Janey O'Riordan

Published in London by Studio Vista Limited
Blue Star House, Highgate Hill, London N19
and in New York by Watson-Guptill Publications
165 West 46th Street, New York 10036
Library of Congress Catalog Card Number 72–97945
Set in 9 on 9½ pt Univers
Printed and bound in Great Britain by
Bookprint Limited, Crawley, Sussex
SBN 289 79724 1

Contents

Introduction 7
What do we mean by abstract? 10
The abstract qualities 18
Finding motifs 24
Making motifs 40
Motif 44
Motifs from collage 45
Motifs from impressing 47
Motifs from collecting 48
Visual exploration 51
Motifs from projecting 52
Motifs from printing 54
Motifs from rubbings 55
Enlarging by squaring-up 56
Motifs from doodles 58
Drips, blots, splashes 60
The camera as aid 63
Found abstract 67
Counterchange 73
Pattern 74
Simplification 76
Drawing as abstraction 79
Can you find them? 82
Application of squaring-up 84
Points of view 86
Ideograph, pictograph, symbol 90
Abstract art and the community 93
Vision 97
Colour 98
Conclusion 101
Further reading 102
Solutions 103
Index 104

Glory be to God for dappled things–
For skies of couple-colour as a brinded cow;
For rose-moles all in stipple upon trout that swim;
Fresh-firecoal chestnut falls; finches' wings;
Landscape plotted and pieced–fold, fallow, and plough;
And all trades, their gear and tackle and trim.

All things counter, original, spare, strange;
Whatever is fickle, freckled (who knows how?)
With swift, slow; sweet, sour; adazzle, dim;
He fathers-forth whose beauty is past change:
Praise him.

'Pied Beauty' by Gerard Manley Hopkins

Introduction

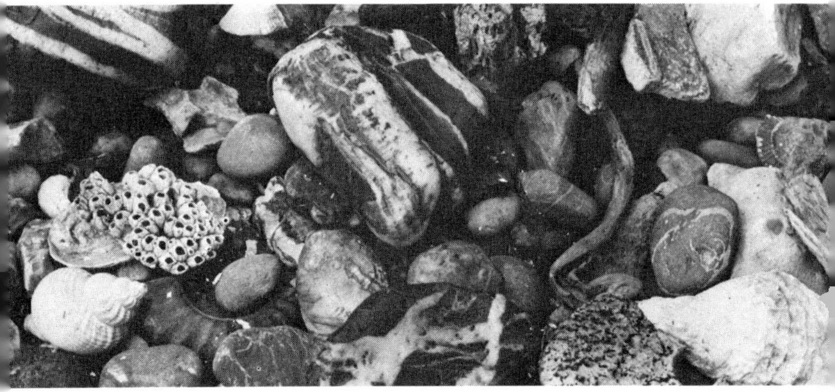

Fig 1

The visitor to 'open' exhibitions of art will be aware of differences between the work of the professional and the non-professional. It seems that these stem mainly from the non-professional's extreme conservatism in choice of subject matter. If a census could be taken of the content of the works on display in exhibitions of amateur art, it would show a preponderance of three types of subject: landscape, still life, and portrait, probably in that order. The amateur is less likely to go in for so-called 'modern art' than his professional colleague. Professional exhibits range much more widely and much more rarely fit into the three narrow categories mentioned above. What does this mean? Why do these differences exist? What, if it comes to that, do we mean by 'modern art'?

Look for a moment at the pictures reproduced in figs 2 and 3. Which is the more modern? The one by Picasso was painted more than fifty years ago. The Welsh landscape was painted recently. This makes nonsense of the word modern when it is applied to these two paintings. Pop Art, Op Art, Surrealism, Constructivism, Cubism, Vorticism and the rest are scattered across the last fifty years in unexpected, non-chronological order. The truth is that each 'ism' and each type of painting is the product of a different 'idea', or way of seeing, or thinking.

All these movements were given labels; and not always by their members. Abstract Art is one of these. Abstract Art is easier to comprehend than some of the others, perhaps because visibly it is closely related to everyday experience. With this in mind it is surprising that more amateur painters do not practise it.

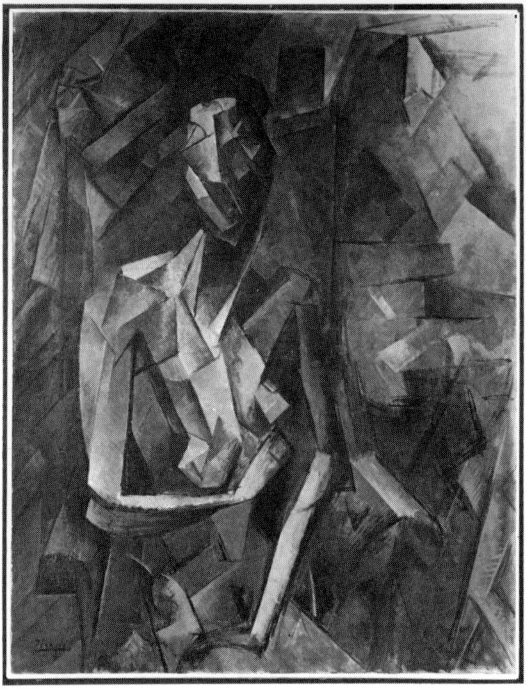

Fig 2 *Seated Nude* by Pablo Picasso *c.* 1910. Tate Gallery, London. © by SPADEM, Paris 1969

What the artist paints, and why he paints it, is more a matter of outlook and motivation than special ability in drawing and painting. Technical skill is fairly evenly distributed throughout the range of artists, from the newest amateur to the most seasoned professional. One of the fundamental differences between the professional and the non-professional is that the trained artist, whether he attended a college of art or whether he is self-taught, is sensitive to all of his environment; not only to conventional landscapes, dishes of fruit, or portrait heads. The trained artist looks with intense visual curiosity at everything, not just at certain types of subject. It is a difference in sensitivity of seeing. The ability to 'see' rather than merely to 'look' is what matters.

Visual sensitivity, the ability to see, can be acquired by visual exploration, by discovery, and by finding. Most readers will recall the pleasure of walks along the beach. The seashore invites exploration of all kinds, and visual exploration plays an important part. We all remember the patterned pebble, the gull's feather, the scoured and bleached Henry-Moore forms of drift-

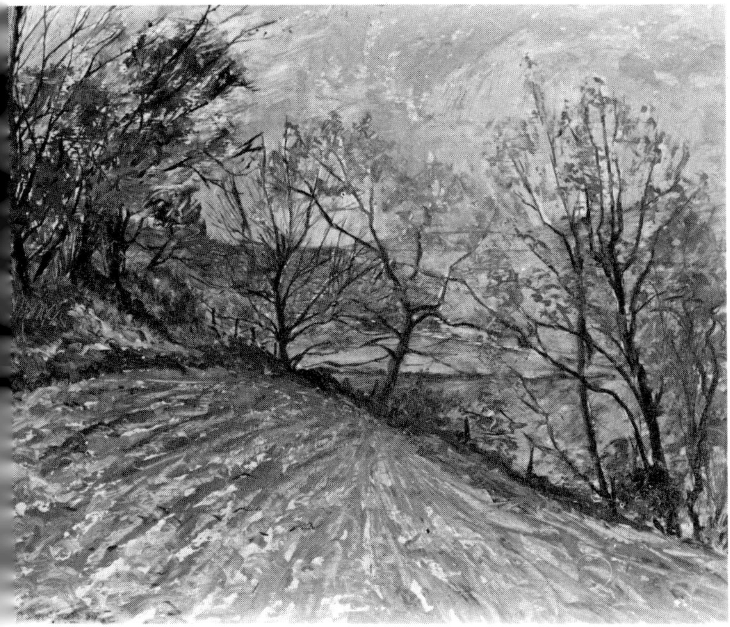

Fig 3 *Welsh Landscape* by Kenneth Jameson. Royal Academy Exhibition, London 1958

woods and sea-defences – things which seem strange and magical, and new every walk we take.

The same sort of magic can be found all around us – in the home, in the garden, the road, the park. . . .

Look at the patterned pebbles in fig. 1 (page 7), and recall the pleasure of holding a pebble in your hand – curiously traced and marked, gleaming wet and smooth. What is it that evokes this pleasure? The pebble has shape, it has colour, it has line, it has pattern, it has form. In artistic terms these are its 'abstract' qualities. Your pleasure in the pebble is a reaction to abstract qualities. If you react to these qualities in a pebble, why should it be difficult to accept them for use in a picture? You are a painter. Why not try using these abstract attributes of your environment as subject matter for your paintings?

You probably found the pebble accidentally. You can find the same sort of pleasurable experience as you found in the pebble, by systematically searching for the same qualities as the pebble had in other places and situations. This is what this book is about.

What do we mean by abstract?

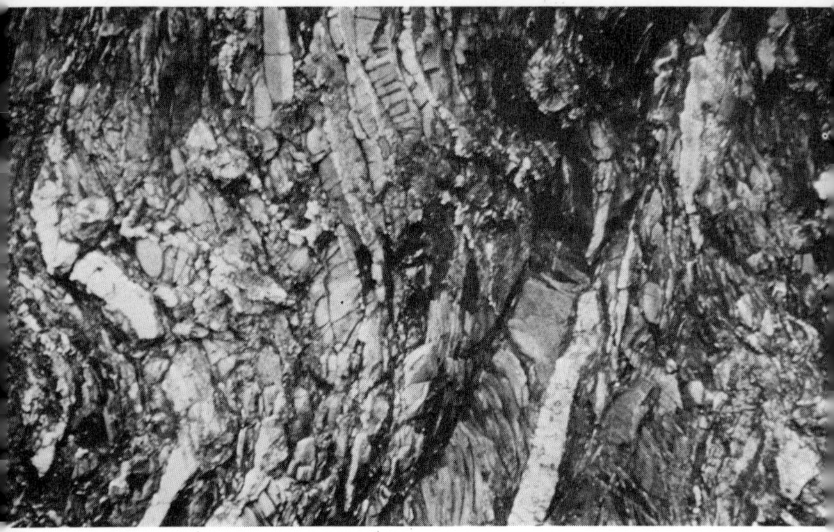

Fig 4

Study the six illustrations on these two pages. Can you easily pick out which are the three photographs of paintings? Of these three can you say which are the two abstract paintings? Try this simple exercise *without* first looking at the solutions. Now check with the solutions on page 103. Did you get it right? See also page 82.

Fig 5

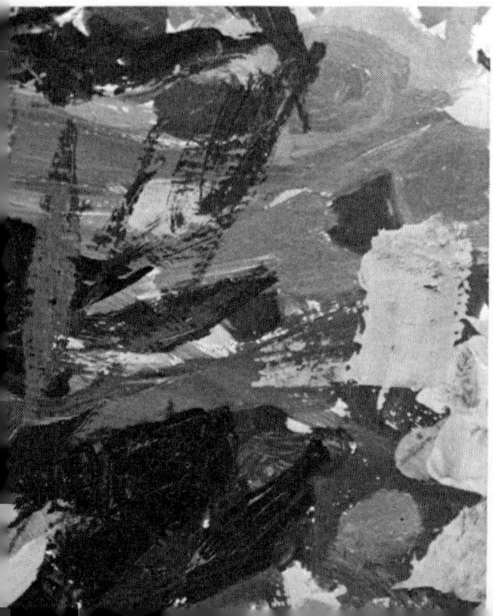

Fig 6

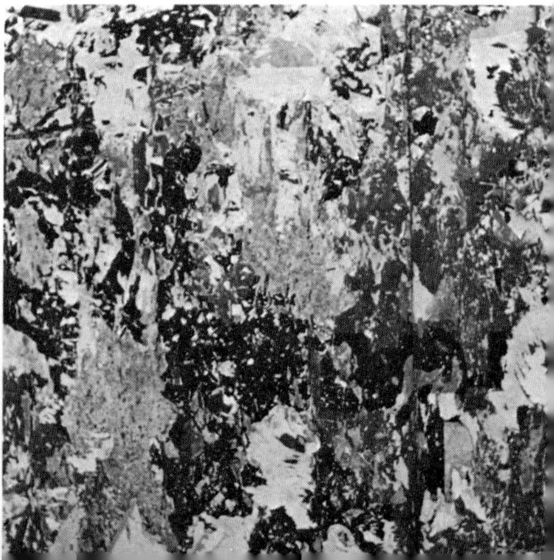

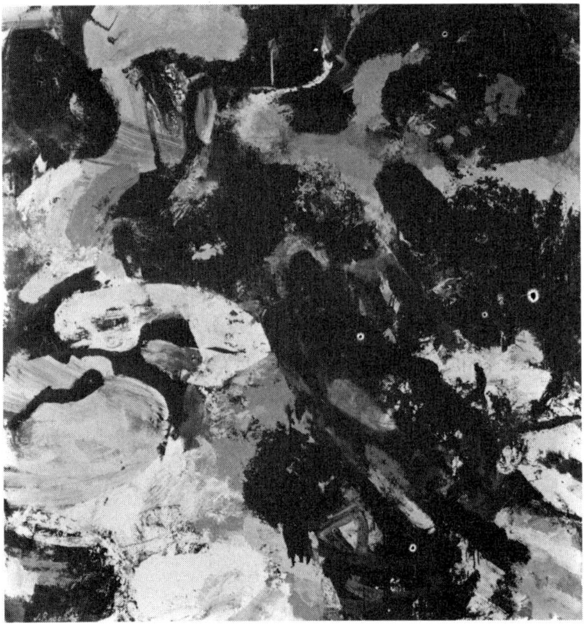

Fig 7

Fig 8

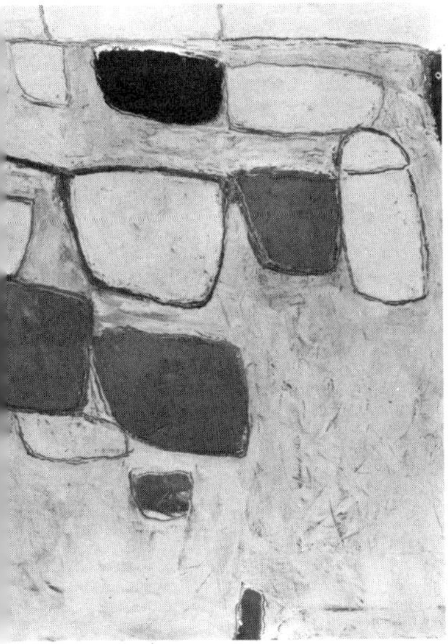

Fig 9

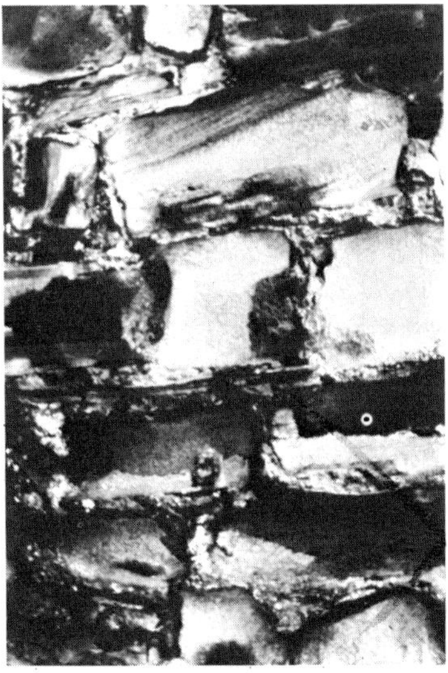

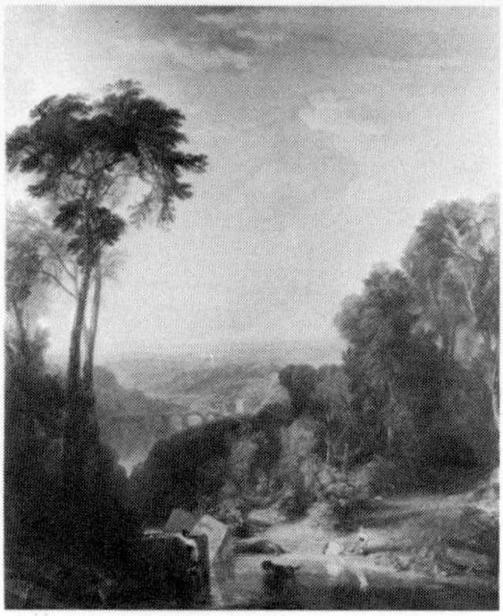

Fig 10 *Crossing the Brook* by J. M. W. Turner. Tate Gallery, London

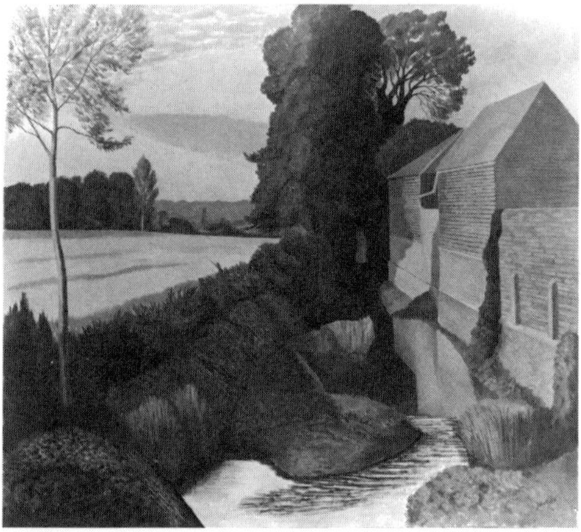

Fig 11 *Mill Buildings, Boxted* by John Nash. Tate Gallery, London

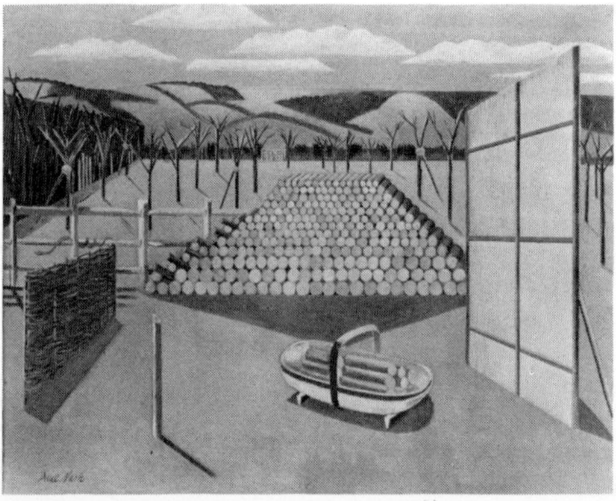

Fig 12 *Landscape at Iden* by Paul Nash. Tate Gallery, London

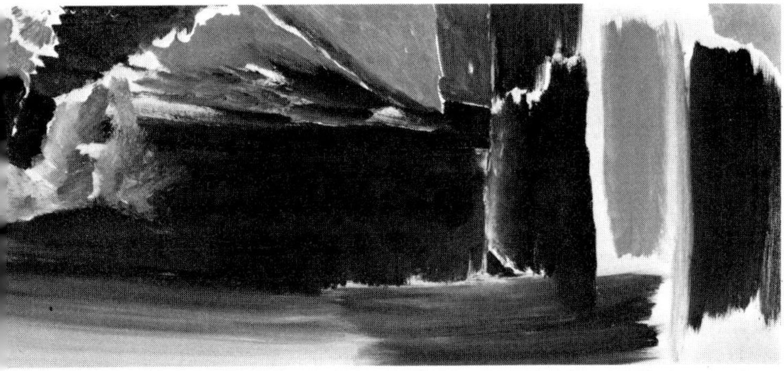

Fig 13 *Woodland, Vertical and Horizontal* by Ivon Hitchens. Tate Gallery, London

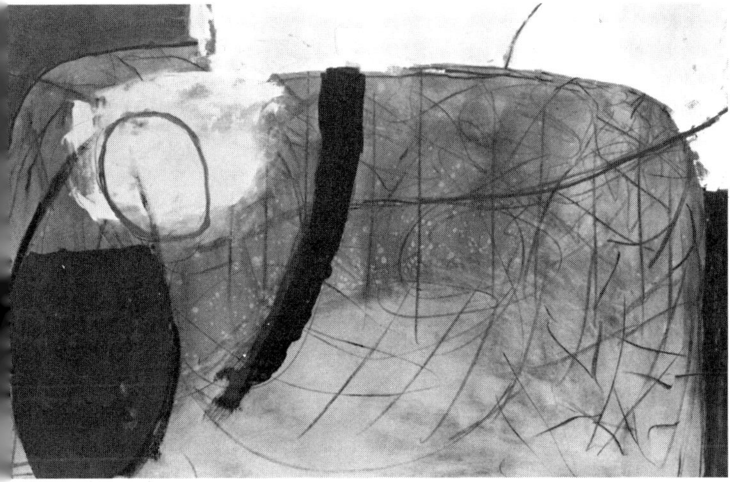

Fig 14 *March 1960* by R. Hilton. Tate Gallery, London

The first of the five pictures reproduced on these two pages, fig. 10, shows its subject in a literal, almost photographic way. The next, fig. 11, differs in that it simplifies the content to some extent. If you study it, you will notice that less detail is included, and that the large masses are made less complex in outline. The third, fig. 12, simplifies the large masses even further, and reduces the three-dimensional parts to simple forms, for example the tree trunks and branches are reduced to cylinders. The shapes in the fourth picture, fig. 13, are much nearer to 'shapes in their own right' than they are to 'shapes representing natural forms'. In other words, the shapes are really an assembly of colours and masses made by the painter, and exist in their own right, almost independent of nature. In fig. 14, the move away from representation is complete. What are we left with? Shape, colour, line, tone, texture, balance, harmony, pattern, design – the same 'abstract' attributes as we saw in the pebble we were discussing earlier, page 9.

Some pictures, like the Turner (fig. 10), although they use abstract qualities, are not abstract at all. On the contrary they are almost photographic. Others, at the opposite end of the scale, are totally non-representational, totally abstract. In between these two extremes there are varying degrees of literalness and abstraction. All painters vary; from barely abstract at all to very, or totally, abstract.

What sort of painter are you? You need to know. Try the following simple experiment.

Collect together as many of your paintings as possible. Stand them round the room, then sit down and study them really closely, if possible as though you were seeing them for the first time. Consider it to be an exercise in self-criticism and self-appraisal. See whether you can decide where you stand in this matter. Are you a literal painter, or a halfway man, or is your work non-figurative? What is the predominant feature in your work? Colour? Texture? Line? Shape? Pattern? Perhaps it is a combination of one or two, or all of these. Which of these attributes matters most to you? Which kind of subject matter attracts you most? Subjects vary in 'abstract' content, from the detailed conventional landscape, still life or portrait to, for instance, the sudden abstract impact of a patch of golden sunlight on a yellow wall, meaning no more than that, telling no story, having no meaning other than the aesthetic shock of luminous gold on yellow. One definition of abstract painting is that it tells no story, has no recognizable subject, points no moral.

But return to fig. 5 (page 10) for a moment. The detail illustrated there was taken from a flower painting. The total work is a fairly literal, somewhat impressionist painting; yet the small detail, in itself, is abstract. I am labouring this point because it is important to realize that all paintings are basically abstract. The eye trained to be sensitive to colour, line, texture, shape, form, tone, pattern, will bring richness to the work, whether the painter works in an abstract way or in a representational one. The insensitive eye can paint a picture. It is unlikely to produce a work of art.

The expressiveness of a representational work of art is the product of its abstract qualities.

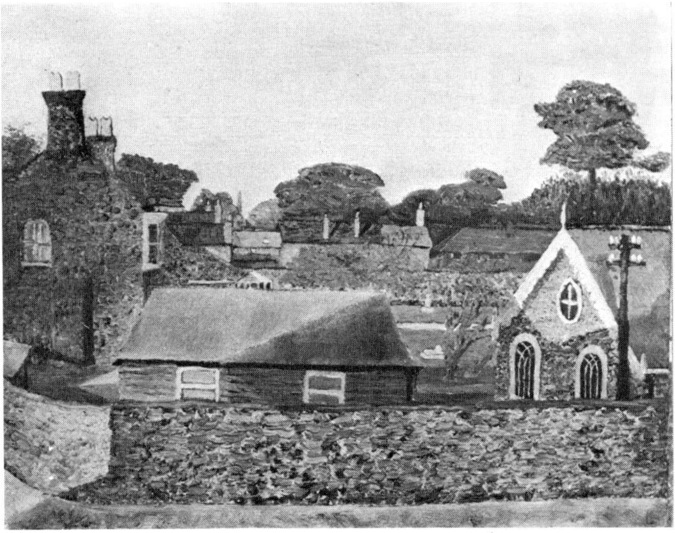

Fig 15 *Low St Agnes Gate, Ripon*, oil painting by a beginner; strong feeling for texture

Fig 16 *Cup and Palette*, oil painting by a beginner; strong feeling for shape

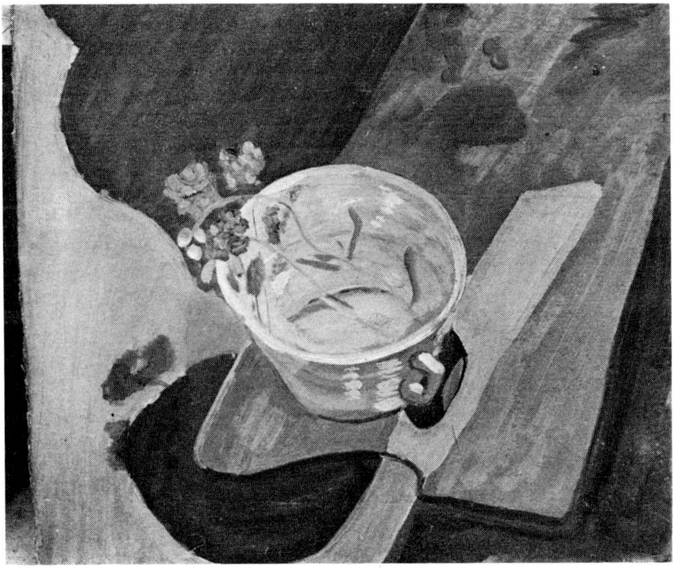

You may never paint an abstract painting as such in your life, but if you make yourself aware of abstract qualities, this will enliven all your work, whether painting, drawing, print-making, design, or any other form of expression.

There are two commonly accepted meanings of the term abstract in art.

One is that method of expression which begins with the abstract qualities of shape, colour, line, and the rest, and which uses these without any reference at all to recognizable subject matter.

The other implies that the artist begins with recognizable visual, or imaginary, forms; and by simplifying them, or extracting motifs from them, produces abstract pictures.

Let us begin by looking at an example of the first of these two alternatives.

The remarkable painting on the next page is by a child aged four. It was produced in a typical situation, in a good infants' (elementary) school, where paints, brushes, paper, easel are always available and ready for use, and where the children may paint whenever they feel like it. The teacher does not suggest, or demonstrate, or interfere in any way.

The child makes his own personal choice of colours. He chooses the colour which attracts him and he paints it on the paper. He puts one patch first, and then a patch of another colour, in another place, where he thinks it looks good.

He chooses the colours he likes.

He puts them where he thinks they look best.

This is abstract expression at its simplest and most direct. You should try doing this, as an exercise, as follows:

Try to forget everything you know about painting. Try to clear your mind of memories of other artists' work. Mix or choose a selection of colours and use only those which evoke a real response in you. Then paint a series of shapes on the paper or canvas relying entirely upon your reaction to their placing, the way they fit together, and whether they look good.

This is a simple exercise, in self-exploration. Its revelations can be profound.

N.B. The quality of the painting shown in fig. 17 may go some way towards explaining the paradox of the occasional very young childs' work which finds its way into professional catalogues. In Britain recently a five-year-old boy's painting was hung in the Summer Exhibition at the Royal Academy.

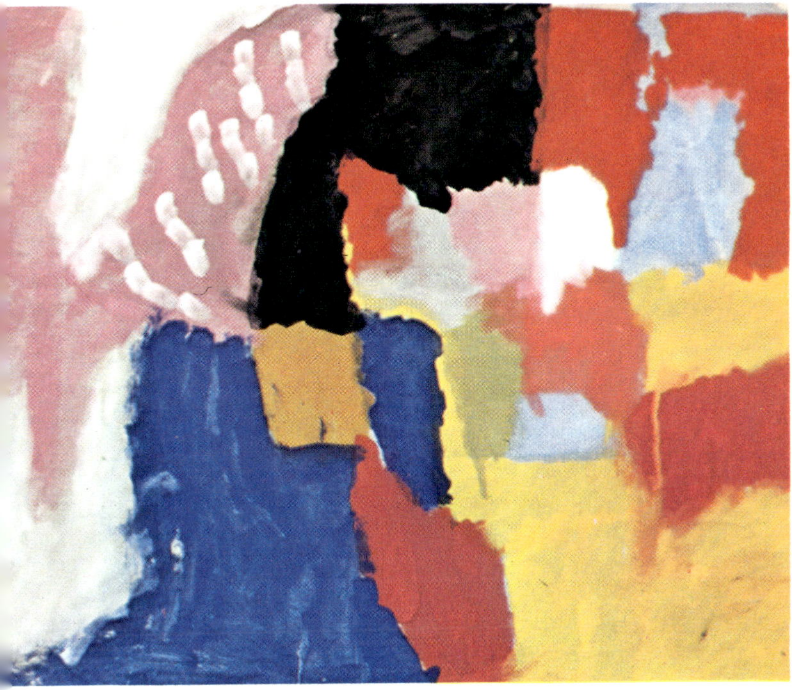

Fig 17

The abstract qualities

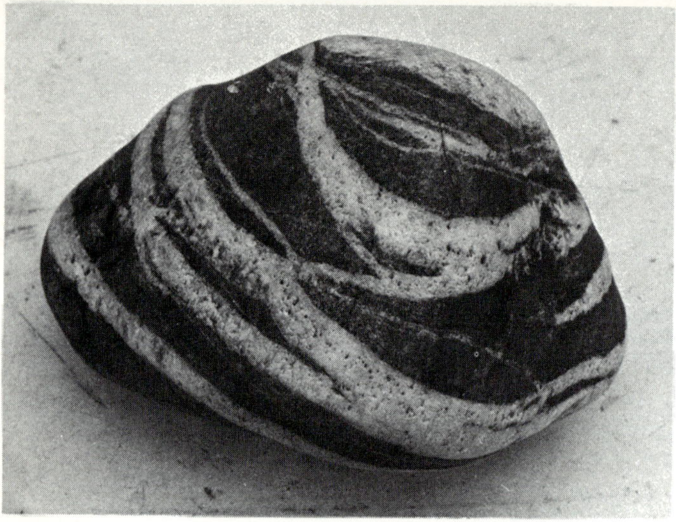

Fig 18   Photograph of pebble

Now let us take a look at the second type of abstract art described on page 16 – the simplifying, or extracting, process. By this I mean 'keeping a sharp eye open' for aspects of our environment which contain elements similar to those we saw in the pebble on the seashore, the properties which made us exclaim 'Look! isn't it fascinating!' As an example, let us look at the pebble above. Examine it closely and see whether you can analyze and separate out its various abstract components. You can see all of them except one in the photograph in fig. 18. The one component you cannot see is colour, so you will have to accept my verbal description. The darker areas are midway between degraded yellow ochre and burnt sienna. By degraded I mean mixed with neutral grey of the same tone or value. The light veinings are subtle, pale pinkish cream. Now let us go on, and in the next few pages we will extract from the pebble as many of its other abstract features as possible. It is more profitable to examine the abstract components *visually*, with the help of illustrations, than to attempt to define them in words.

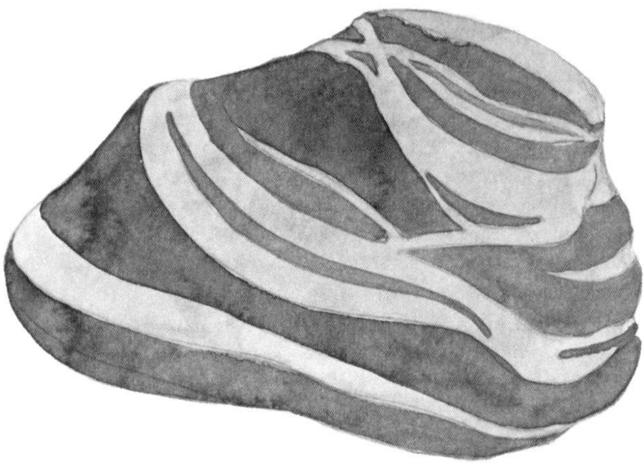

Fig 19 Colour/tone areas of pebble

Colour

I believe colour to be the most important abstract quality. For this reason additional space is given to it later, on pages 98–100.

Colour can be strong or weak, bright or dull, quiet or loud, hot or cold, depressing or exhilarating, primitive or sophisticated, subtle or aggressive. It is abstract, but it is an active component. By itself, in its own right, irrespective of content, it can generate atmosphere, establish a mood.

Fig. 19 shows a map of the colours in the pebble. The dark areas represent the darker ochre-sienna. The light patches represent the pink-cream. The colours are gentle and harmonious.

Tone

Tone is closely related to colour, yet is independent of it. Tone, value as it is known in the U.S., means the degree of darkness or lightness, irrespective of colour. The black and white camera sees everything in terms of tone. Fig. 19 above shows the areas of colour in the pebble; the same fig. 19 also shows the tone.
Fig. 18 is a photograph of the actual pebble.
Fig. 19 is my drawn transcription.
Both should be the same in tone!

Fig 20 Silhouette of pebble

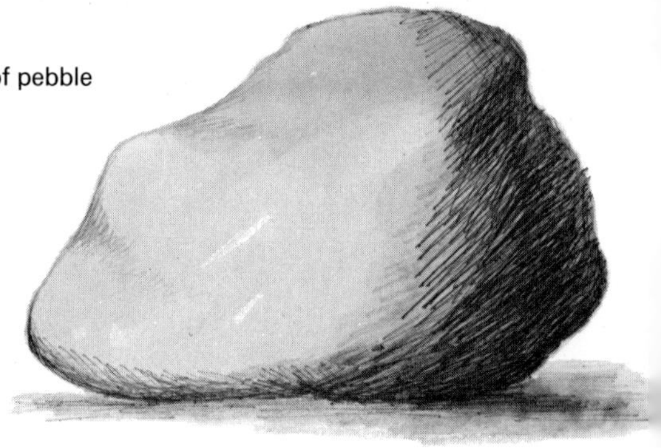

Fig 21 Form drawing of pebble

Shape

The shape, or two-dimensional form, has the strongest visual impact. It is the first, and easiest, abstract quality of the pebble to be comprehended.

Silhouette, or two-dimensional outline shape, is the visual reference by which man recognizes his fellow men and the components of the world in which he lives.

Form

Form can be said to be the three-dimensional version of shape – the solid as opposed to the silhouette. In the case of the pebble – the ovoid as opposed to the oval.

Pattern

The inherent pattern in the pebble is produced by, 1 the division of the total area into minor clearly defined areas and 2 a difference

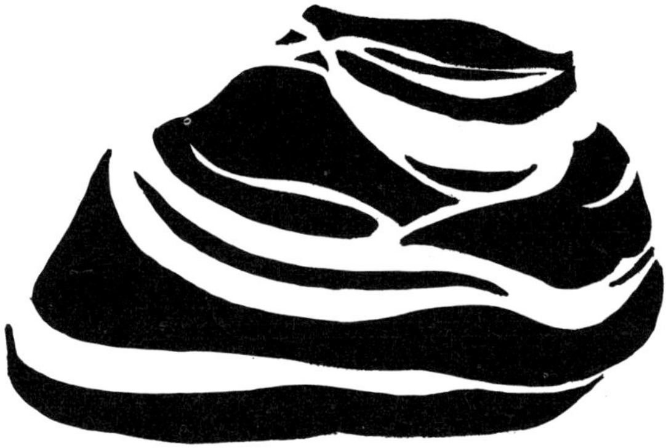

Fig 22 Pattern abstract of pebble

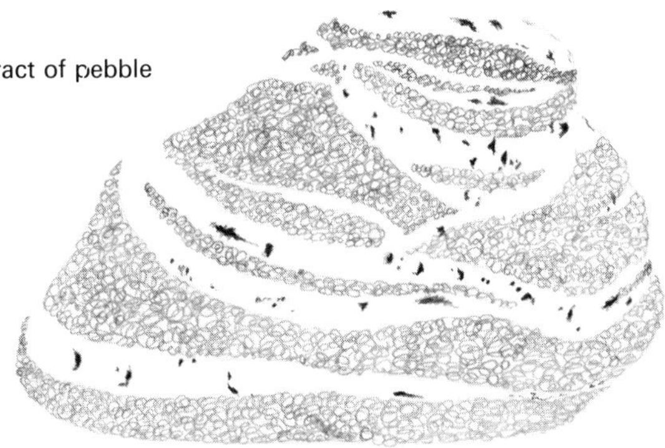

Fig 23 Texture of pebble

in tone between one minor area and another. Because fig. 22 is printed in black and white it gives the strongest tonal difference, and this in turn produces the maximum pattern effect.

What visual image comes into your mind at these words: zebra, gingham, tortoise, butterfly-wing, leopard, chess board?

Texture

Texture, as the artist understands it, is the surface quality of objects, their tactile and visual effect. In this pebble the surface of the dark areas is granular. The light areas are pitted.

The quality of texture is produced by the unlimited repetition of similar modules. In the case of the pebble there are two sets of modules, pimples on the dark areas, and minute craters in the light areas.

Knitted sweater, sand, soap-suds, hessian (burlap), snakeskin do these words evoke a texture image in your mind?

Merely to *look* at texture is not enough; feel it, preferably with your eyes closed.

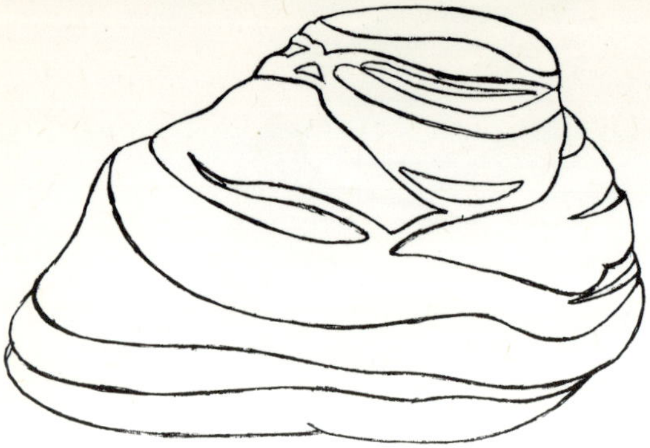

Fig 24 Line abstract of pebble

Line

Line is a convention used by the artist, amongst others. There is no such thing as a line in nature. The line of the horizon is not a line at all. It is the far boundary, the apparent edge, of the sea, or the bottom edge of the sky. The lines in our pebble are the description or the definition of the boundaries between the dark sienna coloured areas and the light cream areas.

Line, or outline, is an abstract way of defining an object. It is also frequently used as a decorative device in its own right, for instance chasing on silver and precious metals.

Drawing could be said to be abstraction in linear terms (see page 79).

Rhythm and harmony

In the preceding few pages we have looked separately at the main abstract qualities. When we make a work of art we combine one or more of them together. We say we *compose* a picture. Composition in art means arranging the various parts. In an abstract picture we arrange the abstract parts. It is no good just throwing them together, haphazardly. They must be carefully arranged, so that they look harmonious, so that they relate one to another, so that the total effect is visually satisfying.

The Oxford Dictionary definitions of rhythm, harmony, and balance correlate when they are applied to art. Because these are the *'unseen* abstracts' we can only study their effects. Judgements on their effects can only be subjective. It is possible to develop your sensitivity to these qualities. In order to do this you must look within yourself to see whether you are aware of harmony and balance in works of art. The diagrams on this page will help you towards finding this out. In fig. 25 which of the five thumbnail

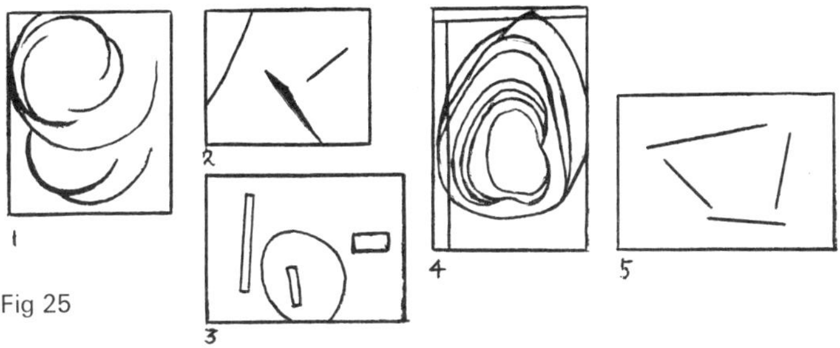

Fig 25

sketches seems to you to be the one in which the components are most correlated, most harmonious? See the solutions on page 103.

Balance

The six diagrams in fig. 26 do not relate directly to the pebble, but they do provide you with an opportunity to test your reactions to visual balance and imbalance. Two of them are off-balance, two are balanced in an unimaginative way, and the other two are varied, balanced and satisfying. Can you identify these three pairs? See the solutions on page 103.

Many artists contend that any one of these abstract qualities is sufficient, by itself, as subject for a painting. Do you agree?

Fig 26

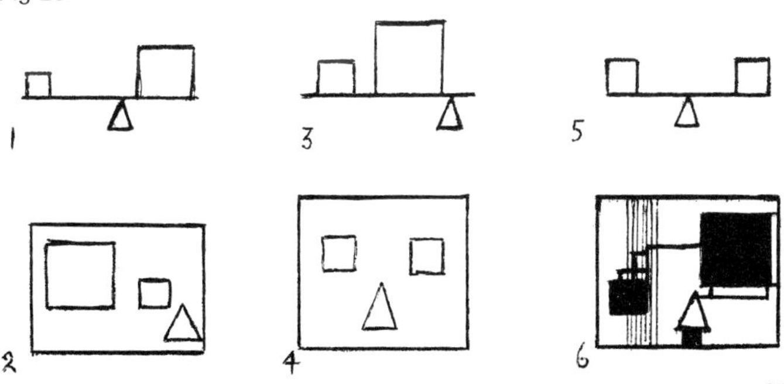

Finding motifs

We used the first few pages of this book to discuss 'abstract' in general terms. We then took a simple example, a pebble, and using this example we identified and separated out the abstract components of colour, tone, shape, form, pattern, texture, line, rhythm, harmony.

I contend that, if your feeling for the abstract qualities of the pebble is strong enough, it would be possible to find in that small compass not just one, but many subjects or motifs, or stimuli for paintings or other forms of creative work.

We used the pebble as an example partly because it happened to be to hand, but mainly because it typifies the richness of visual material which is available in every single aspect of our environment, whether natural or man-made. We live in an 'Aladdin's Cave', surrounded at every turn by exquisite material. All we need do is take what we want. It is there, in full view, all the time. It doesn't matter where you live – in the middle of town, in the suburbs, by the sea, in the mountains, the prairies, in a country village.

Let us see what we can do to explore and find and extract some of this wealth of visual material; and let us see whether it is suitable as 'creative fuel', as motif or as subject matter.

The rest of this book is designed as a series of separate but linked sections. They are not progressive. You can dip where you like. Each one is a development, or a modification, of parts of what we have discussed so far. Each one is complete in itself and invites you to try your hand. Identify, and keep in mind all the time, which of the abstract qualities you are dealing with.

We will take as our starting point an aspect of environment which is available to every human being throughout the whole world, wherever he lives – a wall.

I shall step outside my own front door, and see what we can find.

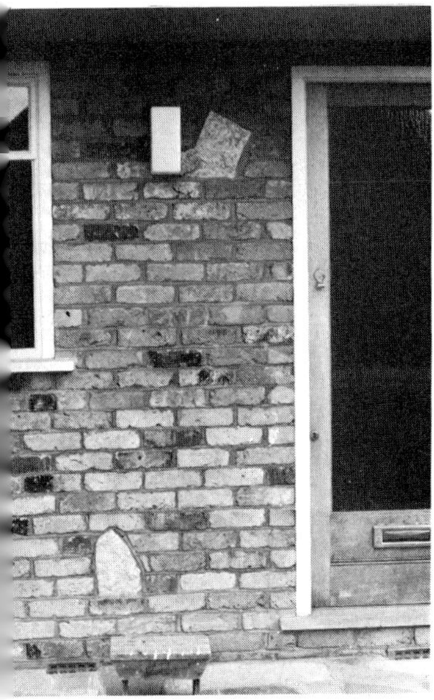

Fig 27

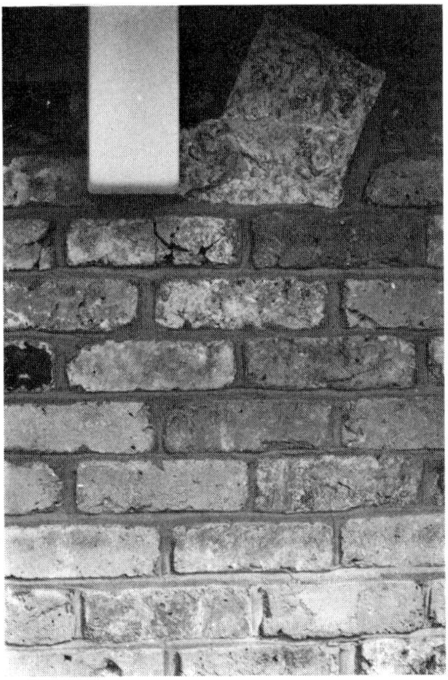

Fig 28

Fig 29

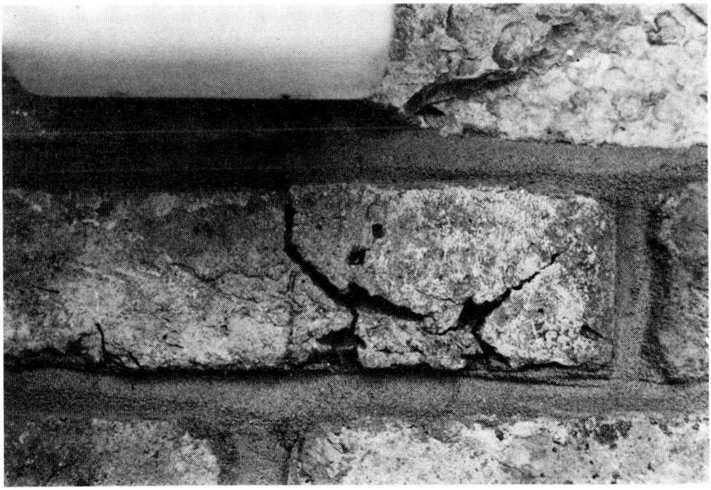

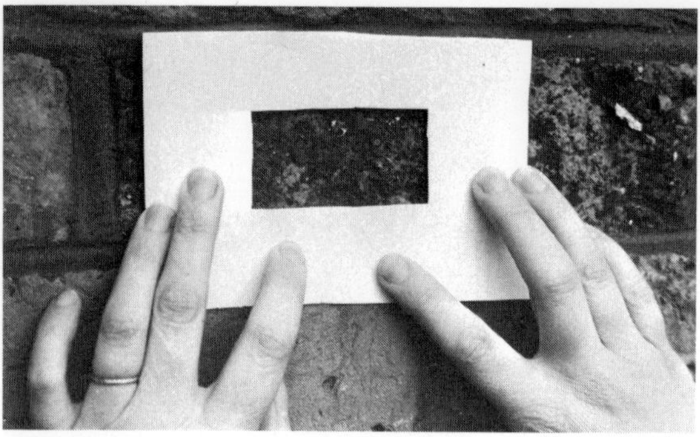

Fig 30 Using a viewfinder to examine other detail before finally deciding on the motif in fig. 31

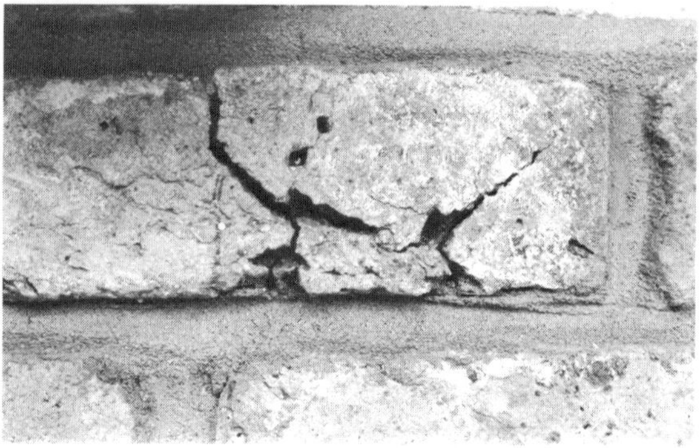

Fig 31 A cracked brick provides a possible motif

Fig 32 The motif, isolated by drawing and modified slightly

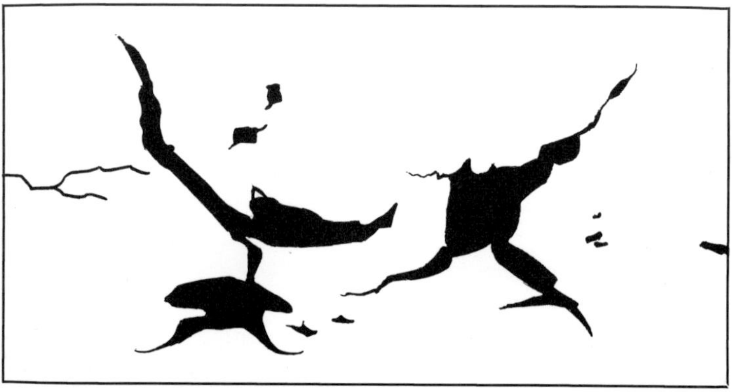

Fig 33 The motif has been transferred to a screen, and is being used to print a large patterned area

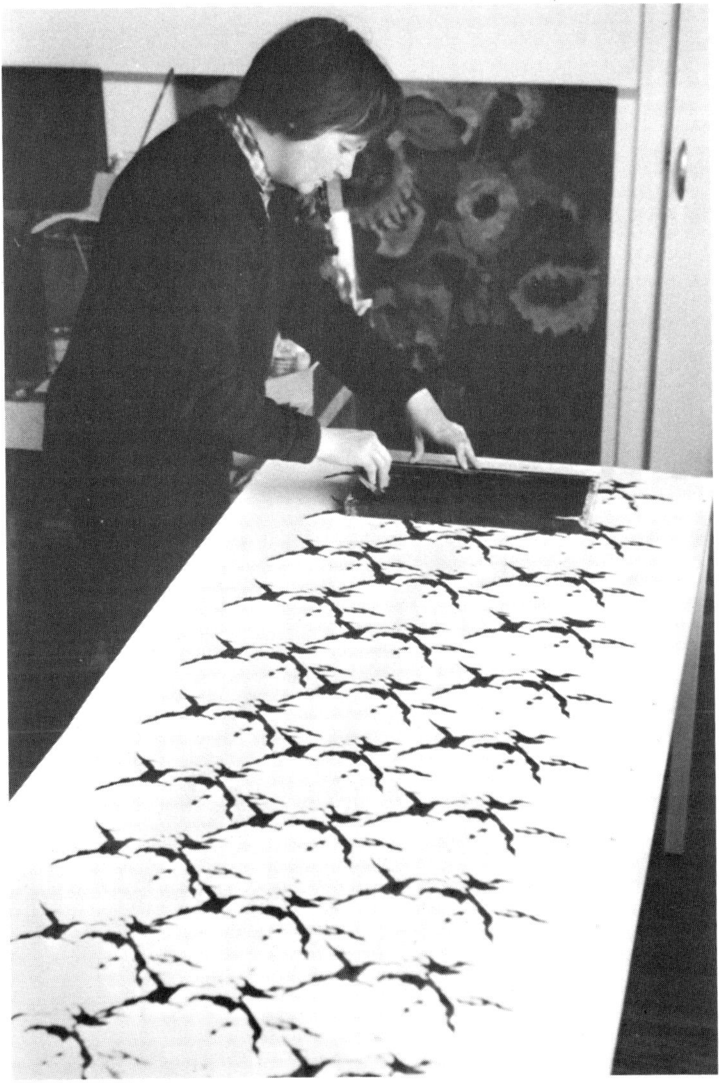

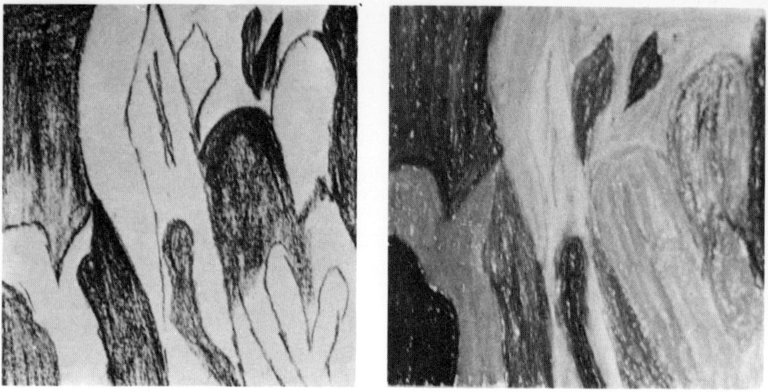

Fig 34

Fig 35

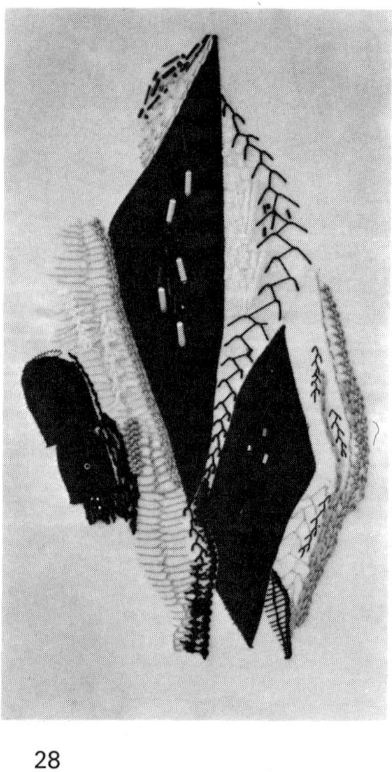

Fig 36

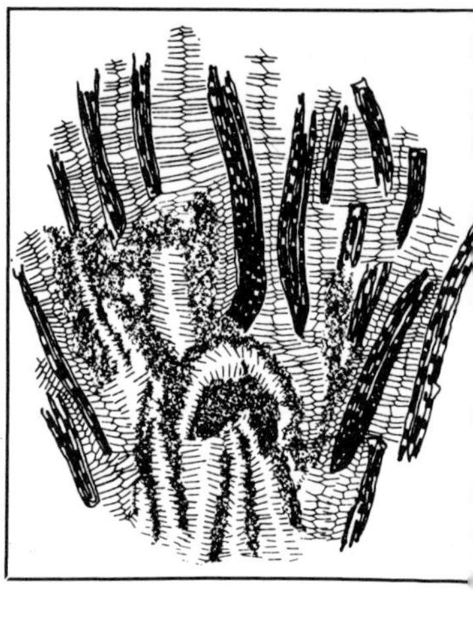

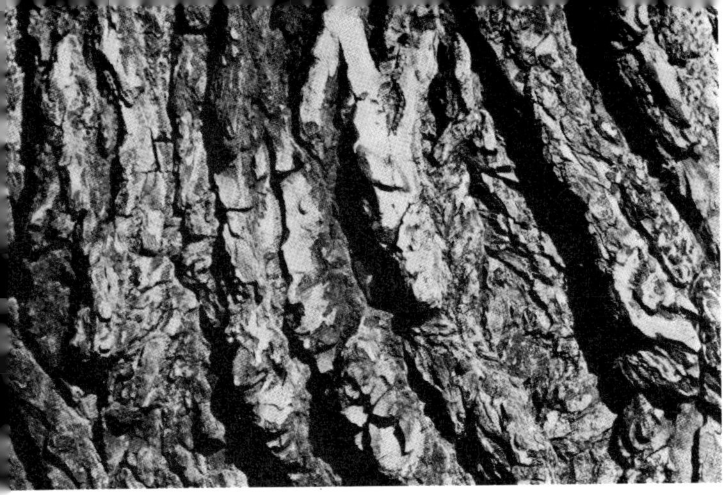

Fig 37

Fig 38

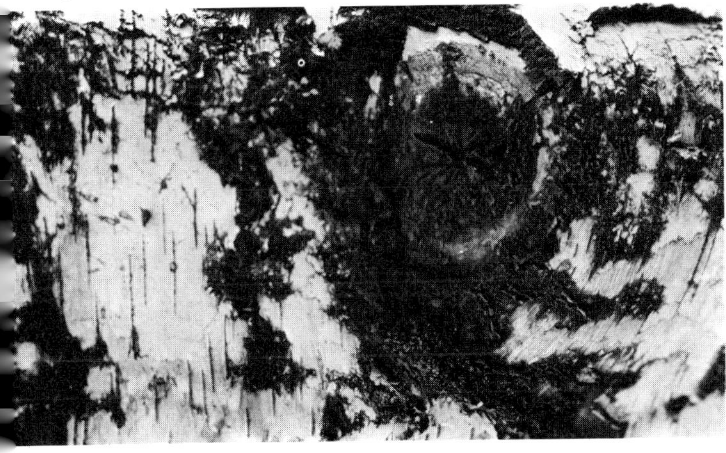

Where else might it be possible to find motifs? Let us take a look at some other aspects of our environment.
The motifs on the opposite page are studies by amateurs, in chalk, appliqué and embroidery. They were abstracted from the plumage of stuffed birds in a glass case.
Trees provide characterful material. Fig. 37 shows a close-toned and richly-textured trunk. Fig. 38 is silver birch – black and white contrasting masses, a ready-made subject. As an exercise, find twelve different trunk motifs. Note them down in your sketch book; or photograph them.

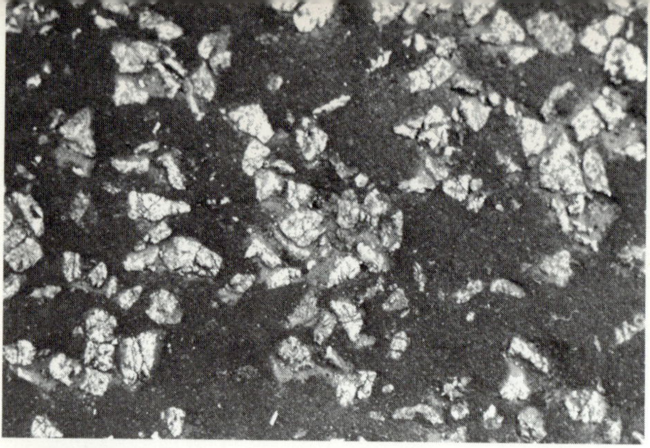
Fig 39

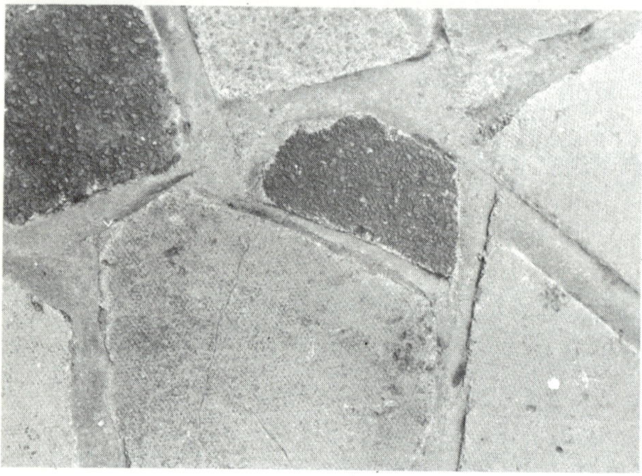
Fig 40

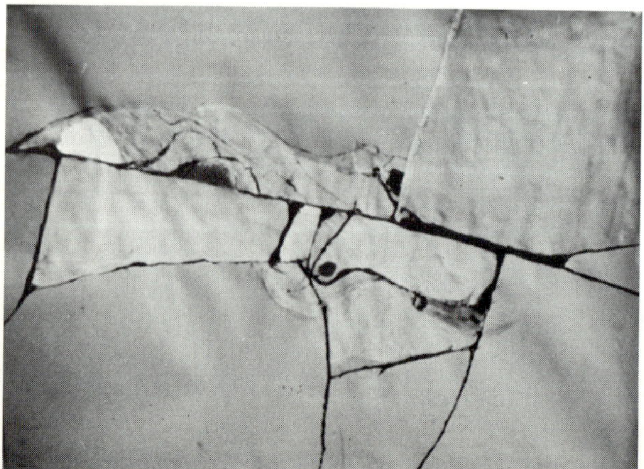
Fig 41

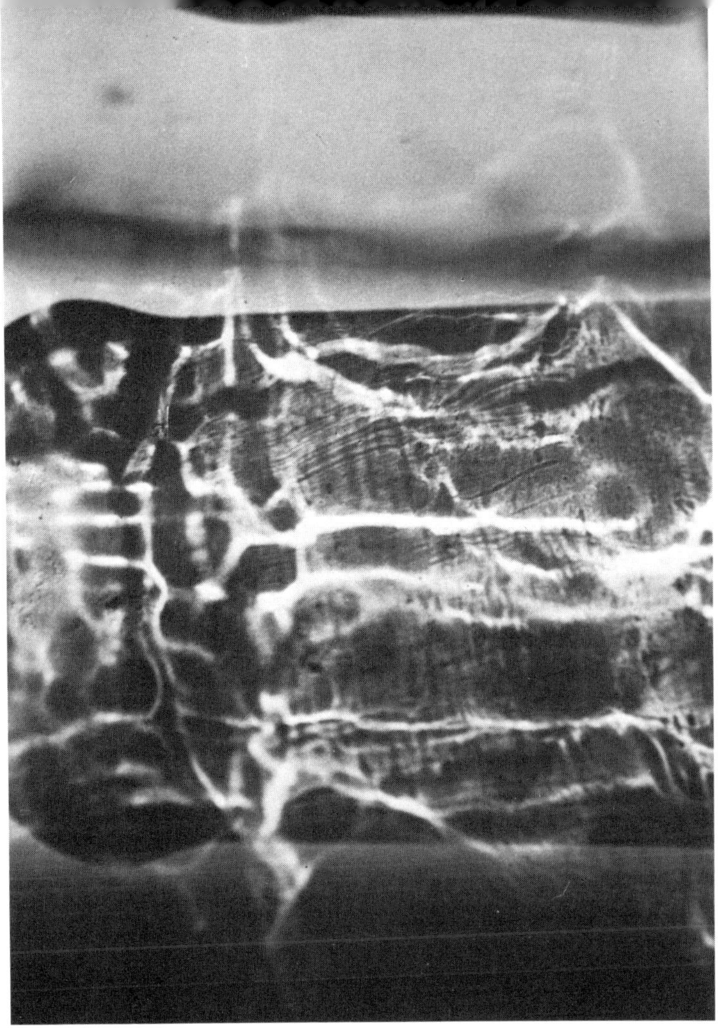

Fig 42

Look down as you walk. Fig. 39 is a photograph of a road surface, fig. 40 a photograph of 'crazy paving'. Fig. 41 is a monochrome study of cracked paving stones on a sidewalk.
Reflections and shadows endow familiar forms with unexpected and strange magic. Above, sunlight shining through a large glass jar containing water. Would you agree that it 'reads' as a mysterious seascape?

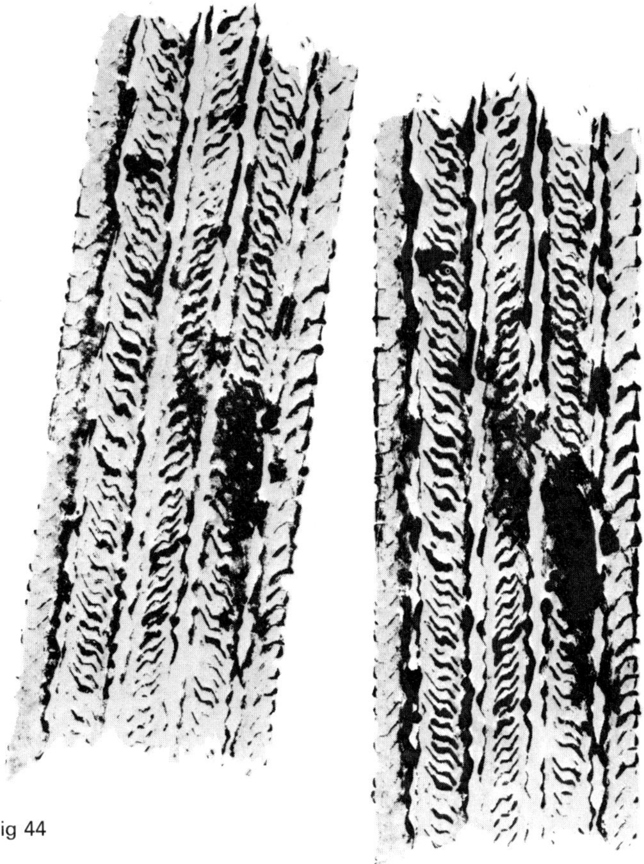

Fig 44

Fig 43 (*opposite*)

Relate these cloud-forms to page 20, especially to fig. 20. Make a series of studies of white shapes in blue (or any other sky-colour) backgrounds, using careful drawings of cloud silhouettes. I spilled some black paint on the garage floor. The car tyre ran through it. I backed the car over a piece of white paper and then ran it forward over the paper again. The two 'prints' so made (above) contain any number of motifs. Find a few with your view-finder (see page 39).

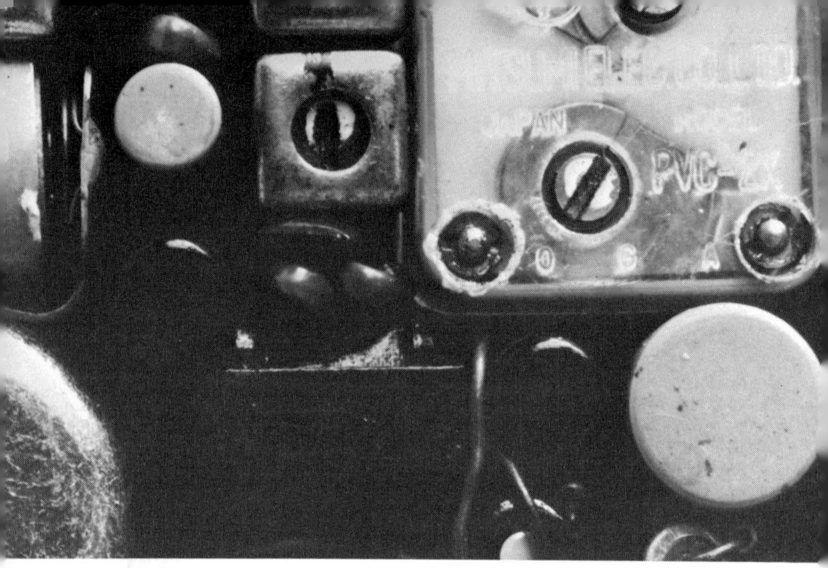

Fig 45

Fig 46

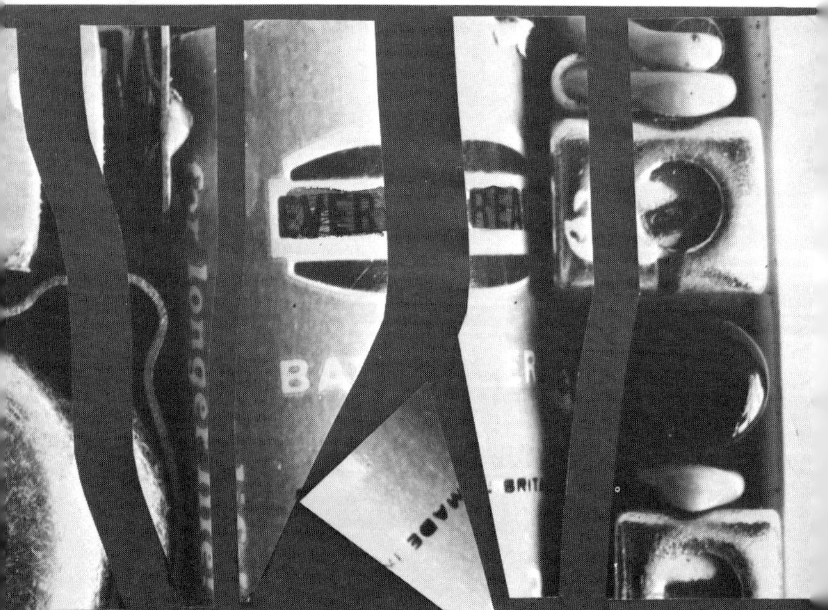

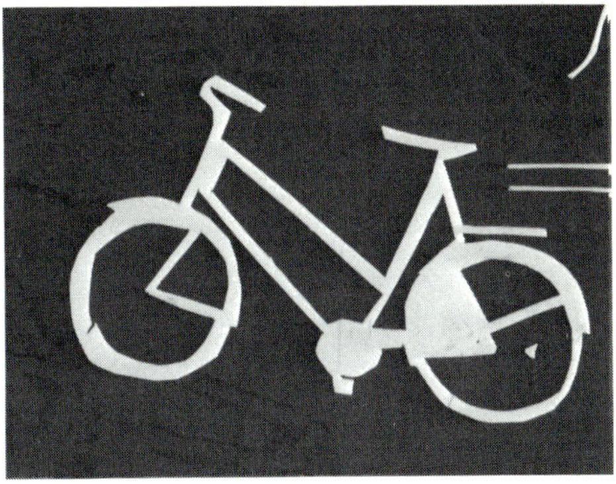

Fig 47

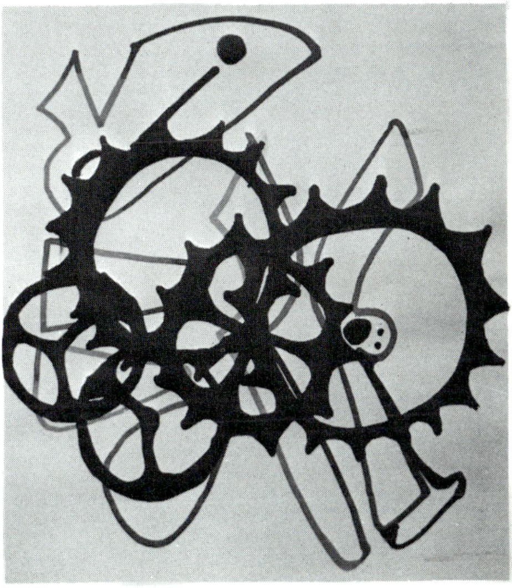

Fig 48

Electronic equipment has a visual character of its own – delicate, fragile and jewel-like. Fig. 45 is a close-up of a pocket transistor radio set interior, fig. 46 a 'sectionalized' version of a similar photograph.

Fig. 47 is a study in 'shape' by a schoolboy aged sixteen. The white lines of the bicycle are the white underneath paper showing through. All the dark shapes, corresponding to the main shapes of the bicycle, were cut out separately and stuck on top of the white paper. You should try this intriguing exercise. Fig. 48, bicycle shapes, black ink drawing by a girl aged nineteen.

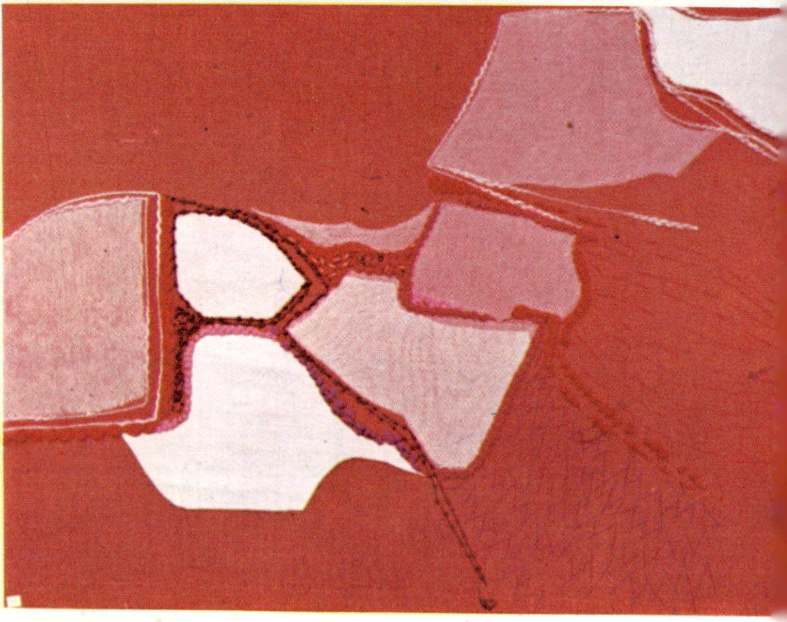

Fig 49 Red abstract embroidery

The original of this red embroidery panel is four feet by three. Notice how the outline rectangle is broken up into nine major shapes, all of which vary in tone and in texture. Note also the skilful use of variously-textured stitchery to enrich certain passages. This panel depends for its effect almost entirely on abstract qualities. The colour is emotive. Can you imagine what the starting point was? Turn to page 103 for the explanation.

Two photographic studies of the same 'between shapes' in a group of sunflowers, one study close-up. I find this subject powerful, exciting and paintable. The fact that they are sunflowers is hardly important at all. It is the shapes, as shapes, the greens and the textures which fascinate me. This is a good example of 'abstract in nature'. The garden is full of such material.

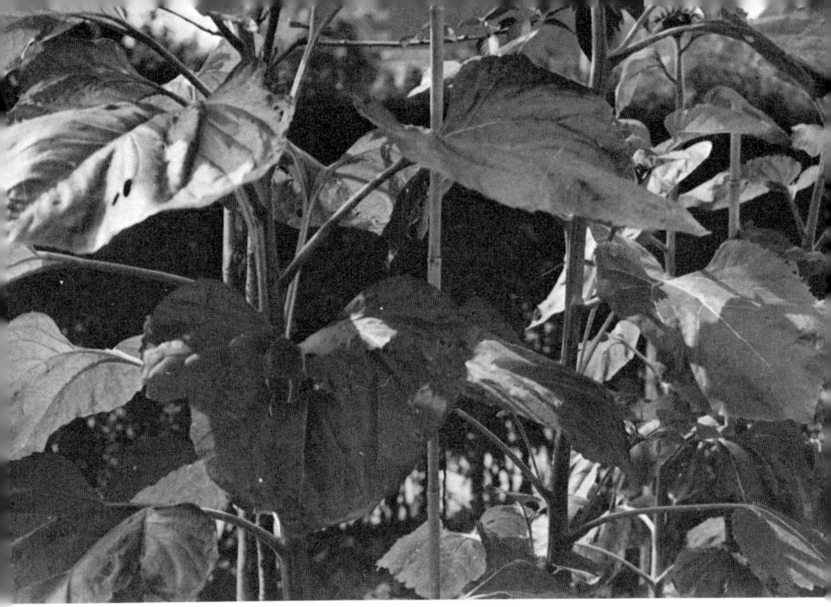

Fig 50

Fig 51

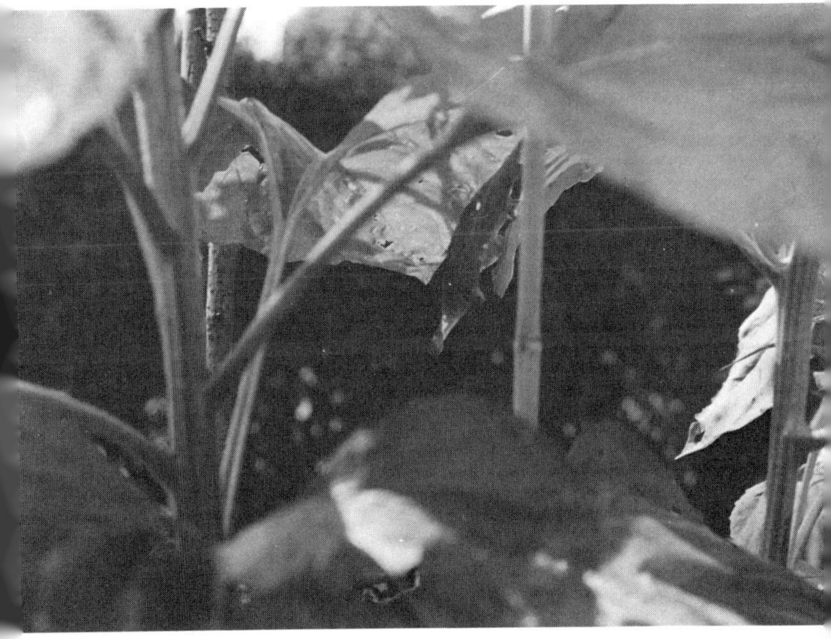

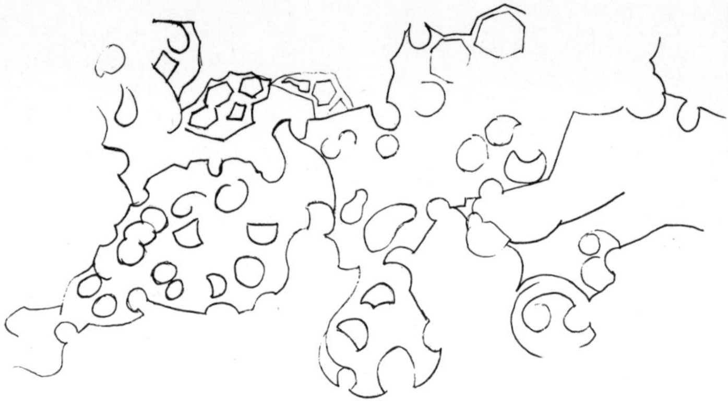

Fig 52 Drawing from illustration below

Any beach teems with evocative forms. Sea-creatures produced the intricate structure below by perforating a buried tree-bole, which is part of a prehistoric submerged forest on the coast of Cardiganshire, Wales.

Some artists work 'from cold'. By this I mean they look within themselves for ideas to use. Others find it more exciting to search and explore and select and modify and develop themes to

Fig 53 Sandworm piles

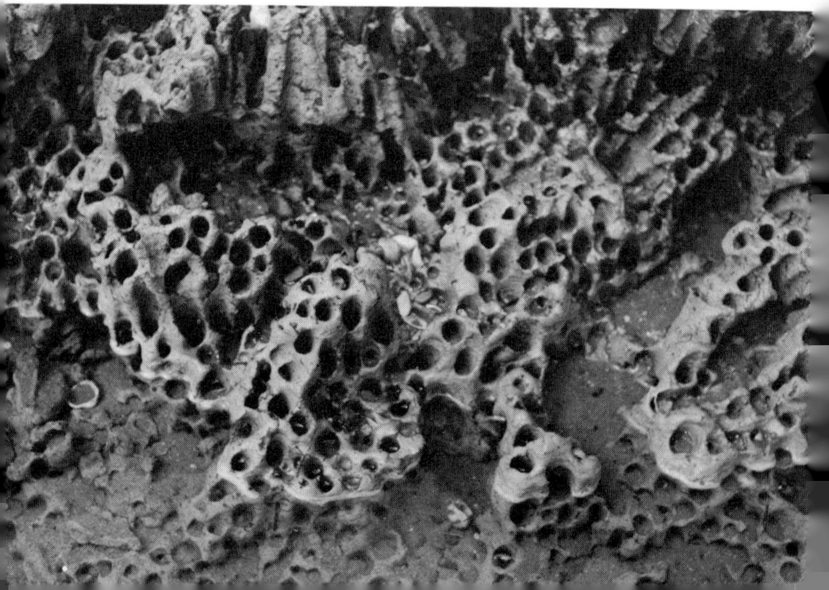

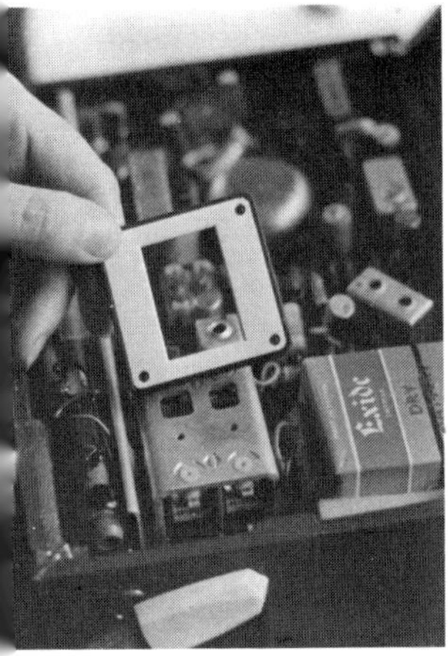

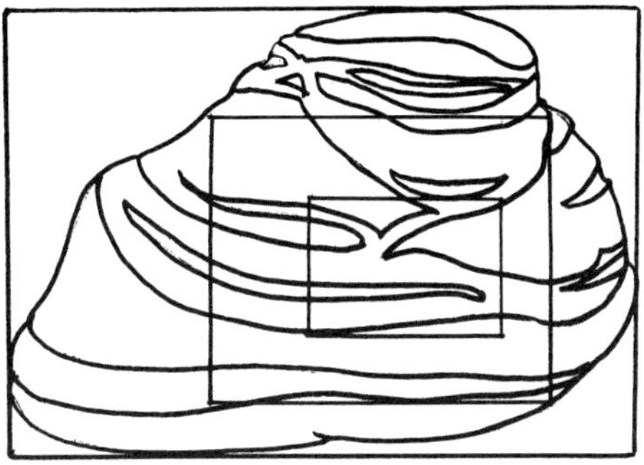

Fig 55 Three different viewfinder sizes give three different motifs

Fig 54 Viewfinder in use

be found in the external environment, whether natural or man-made.

The last fourteen pages have been used to show that 'magic' subject matter exists all around us. The haphazard sequence of the list we have been looking at is deliberate. It was designed to show that material for artistic expression, in any medium, is there for the taking. All we have to do is to see it, to isolate it, and to extract it.

The best aid to isolate that part which interests us is the viewfinder I have talked about. Any piece of board or cardboard with a rectangular hole cut in it will do. As an experimental exercise cut a number of viewfinders with holes of varying proportions and appropriate size, and go back over the last fourteen pages and search over the examples illustrated. See whether you can isolate areas of interest in the illustrations. Then take your viewfinder round the house, and the garden, into the local junk-yard. Search the factory wall. Take it with you on your favourite walk through the woods, or by the river, or in the park.

One very important note to close this section. All the above examples have been of *finding* abstract motifs, from material already in existence. In the next section we are going to examine ways of *making* abstract motifs. In other words, we are going to move a little nearer to the position of 'starting from cold'.

Suggested sizes for holes in viewfinders:

$\frac{1}{2}$ in. $\times \frac{3}{4}$ in.	1 in. $\times 1\frac{1}{2}$ in.
2 in. $\times$ 3 in.	4 in. $\times$ 6 in.

An empty 35 mm. plastic slide frame makes a handy viewfinder, see above.

Making motifs

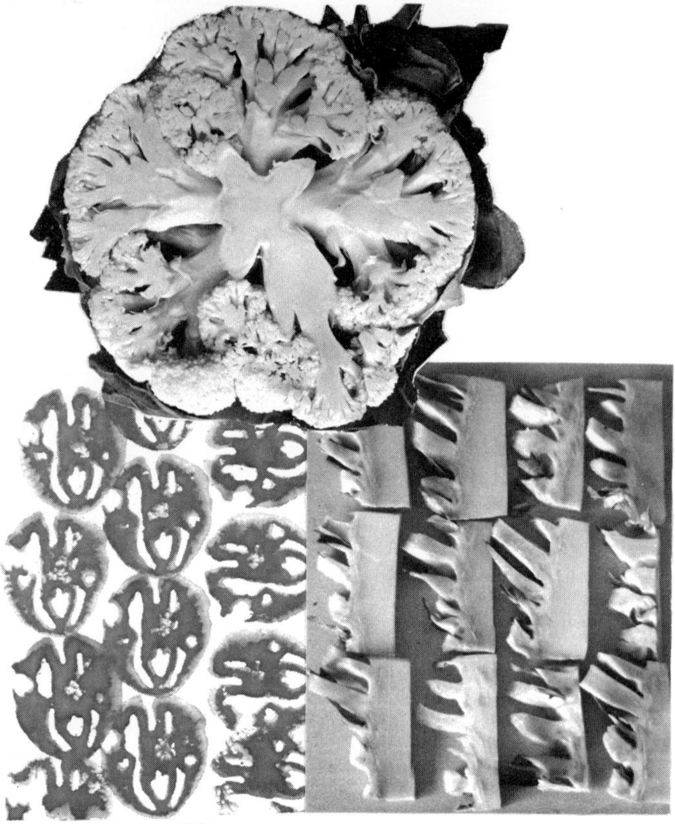

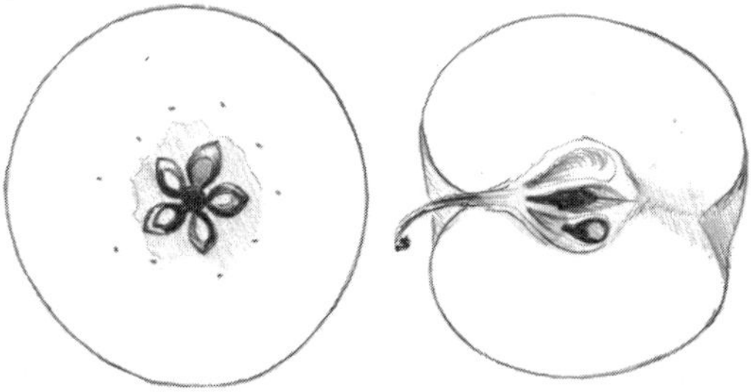

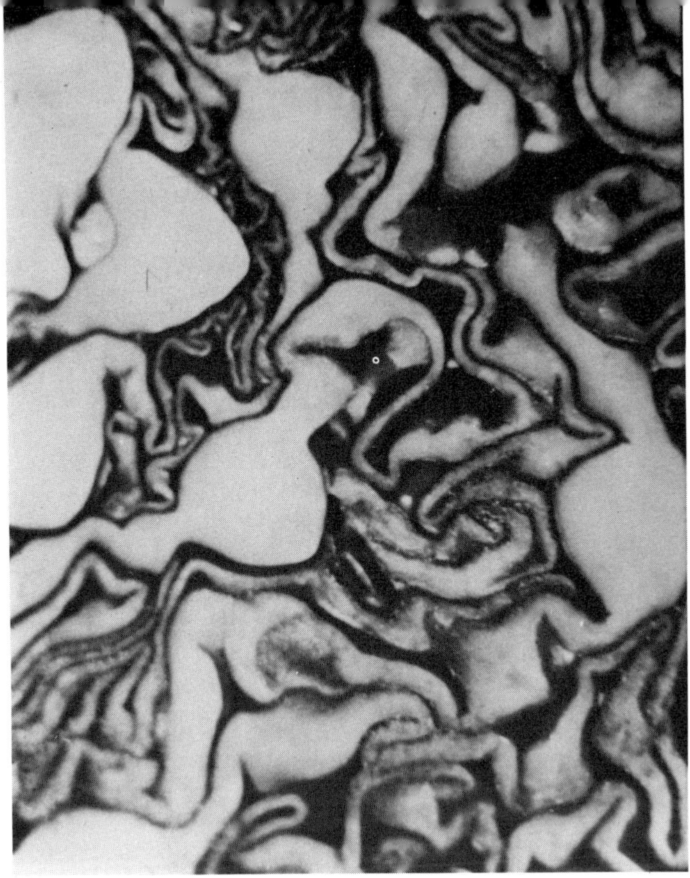

Fig 57 Section of red cabbage

Fig 56 (*opposite*) Montage of 'sections' – drawings, prints and photographs

Some aspects of our environment are universally present but not apparent until some human agency takes a hand; by, for instance, cutting open the cauliflower, the apple, the peach-stone, the cabbage stalk; by tearing and sticking materials, by assembling, by impressing patterns, textures, shapes on surfaces; by projecting natural forms; by printing; by off-setting; by doodling, and so on. Examples of some of these processes are shown in the next thirty or so pages.
Run a small viewfinder over this pattern of a red cabbage cross-section and see what motifs you can find. Then try it with the real thing.

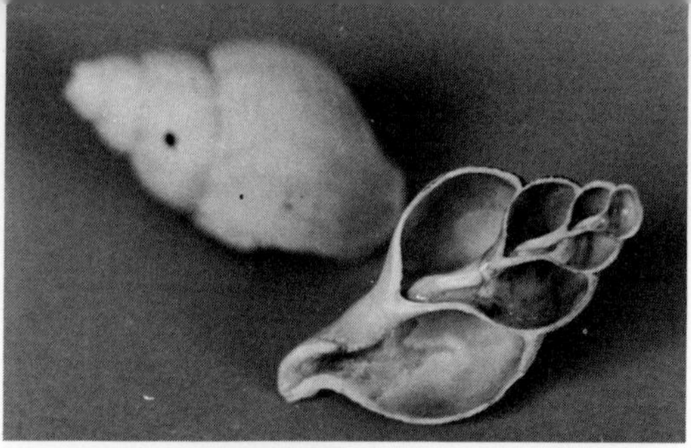

Fig 58

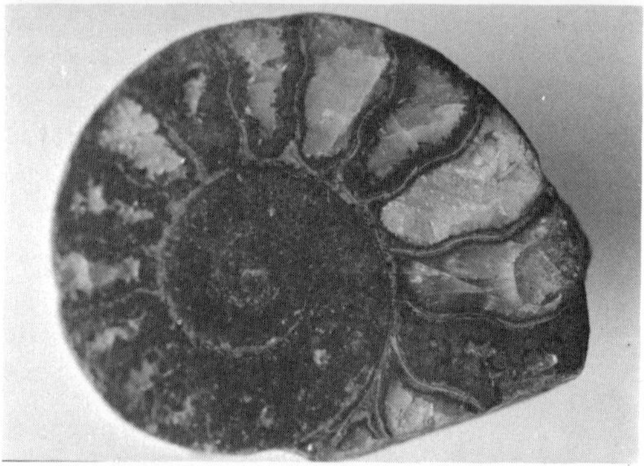

Fig 59

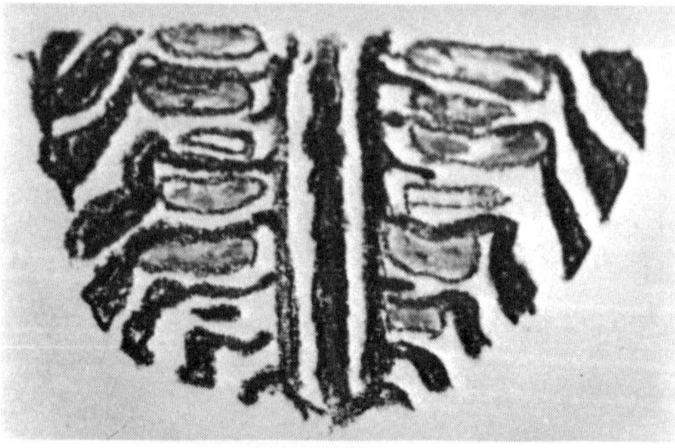

Fig 60

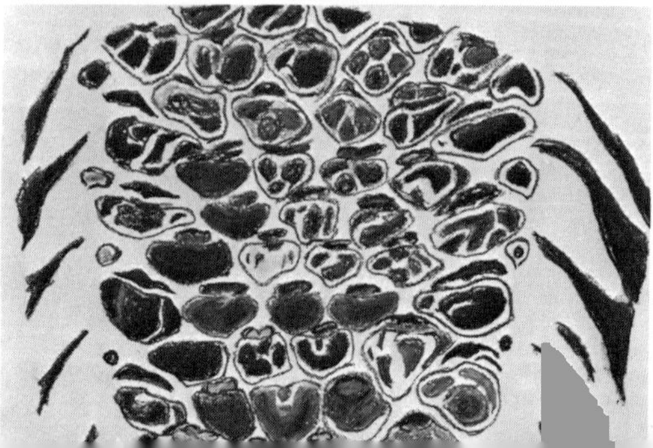

Fig 61

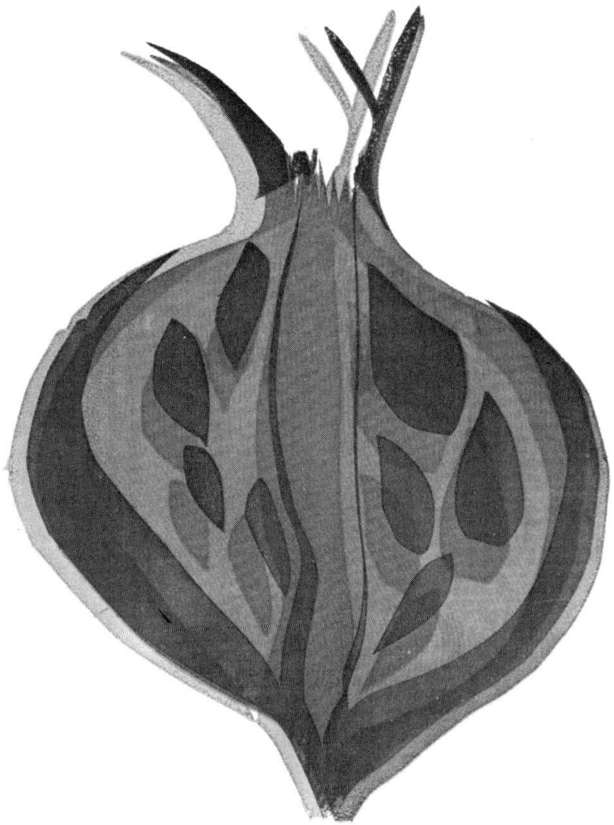

Fig 62

Sections of a fossil ammonite, a sea-shell, and fir-cones provide visual material to draw. Some of them can be used as blocks – i.e. tools to print with.

Do you recognize which natural form provided the section, and hence the abstract shapes, for the design shown above? If not, turn to page 103 for the answer.

This design is a remarkably fine screen print by Jonathan Masters, aged twelve years. It is a good example of the way an abstract motif can be adapted to any medium – painting, drawing, print techniques, pottery, fabric design, and the rest.

So take a look inside your next melon, marrow squash, pomegranate, cucumber, green pepper, aubergine (egg plant), pineapple.

Motif

The word motif has acquired a somewhat narrow meaning. Embroiderers, for instance, speak of a floral motif, meaning a formalized flower design used as a decorative element within a design scheme. When Cézanne spoke of 'setting out to find the motif', he had something quite different in mind. He was thinking in terms of 'trigger-mechanisms'. In the creative arts, particularly music, painting, design, and to some extent poetry, the motif is the trigger mechanism, the starting point. Motif, motive, motivation, are linked words. The connection between them is related to germinal ideas. Motive is the central impelling concept which starts things off. Motivation is the energy at the centre of an act, or an activity, which starts it off and then keeps it going.

There is a difference between 'subject' and 'motif' in our present context. A subject presents itself to the imagination of the artist as a complete entity; for instance the military hero with uniform and medals whose portrait has to be painted! A motif, on the other hand, may be no more than a few accidental marks – texture on a bird's wing, cracks in a wall, a square inch of wood-grain pattern.

The motif, in our context, is an idea, generally a visual idea, strong enough to set our imagination working. It is the seed from which the complete work grows. The motif can be a shape, a line or lines, a texture, a tone, or a natural or man-made pattern. The motif is a germ capable of being organized into a meaningful work of art, or capable of being modified, or developed, or repeated, or enlarged, or combined with other elements.

The motif catches the eye. As soon as we see it, if it contains enough visual interest, it engages our attention. We muse over it and imagine it being enlarged or translated or changed. In other words, as we look, it activates our imagination and we become involved with it.

Every motif is potentially a work of art.

Most of the sections in this book are devoted to showing ways of finding, assessing and developing various kinds of motifs.

I have explained my interpretation of the term 'motif' so that my personal concept of the term will be clear. The word has been used several times already, and will be used many times more before we reach the final page.

The motif provides the artist with his motive and with his motivation.

Motifs from collage

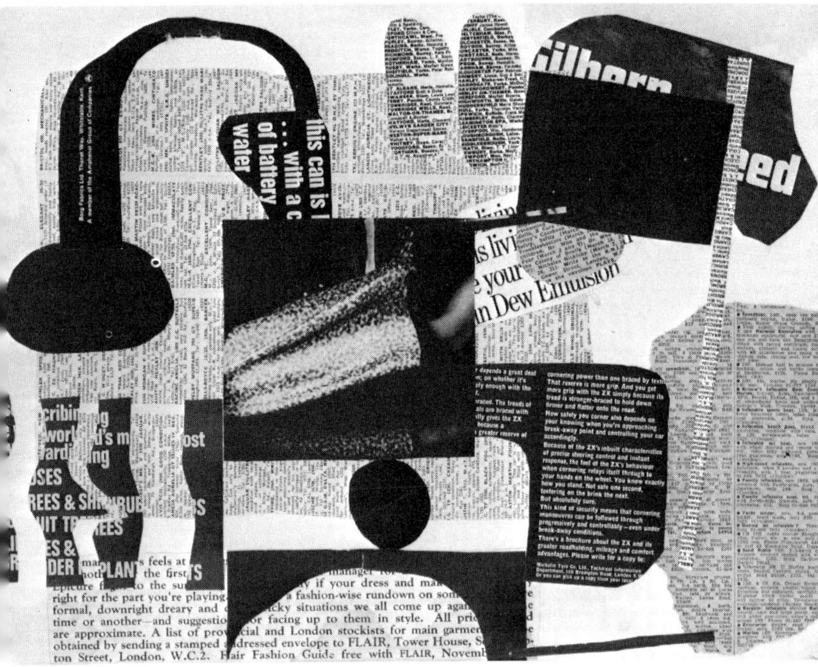

Fig 63 Juggled newspaper abstract

Test yourself by taking a sheet of paper (about 30 in. × 20 in.), some old newspapers and a pot of paste. Cut, or tear, a dozen 'shapes' from the newspapers, varying the print textures, the tones, and the outline shapes as much as possible.

Pin (thumbtack) the large paper to a board and lie it on a flat surface. Experiment by moving the newspaper shapes about, separating, overlapping, watching critically, until you arrive at an arrangement which looks good to you. Then paste the pieces into place and put a lathe frame round. Hang it where you can see it all the time. See whether you can live with it, or whether certain parts begin to worry you. If the worrying parts become too visually irritating, try to decide what the source of irritation is. Is it that the shapes are too big, too small, to dark, too light? Do they unbalance the total design? Are the lines of the offending pieces too straight, or too jagged, to fit with the lines of the other pieces; in other

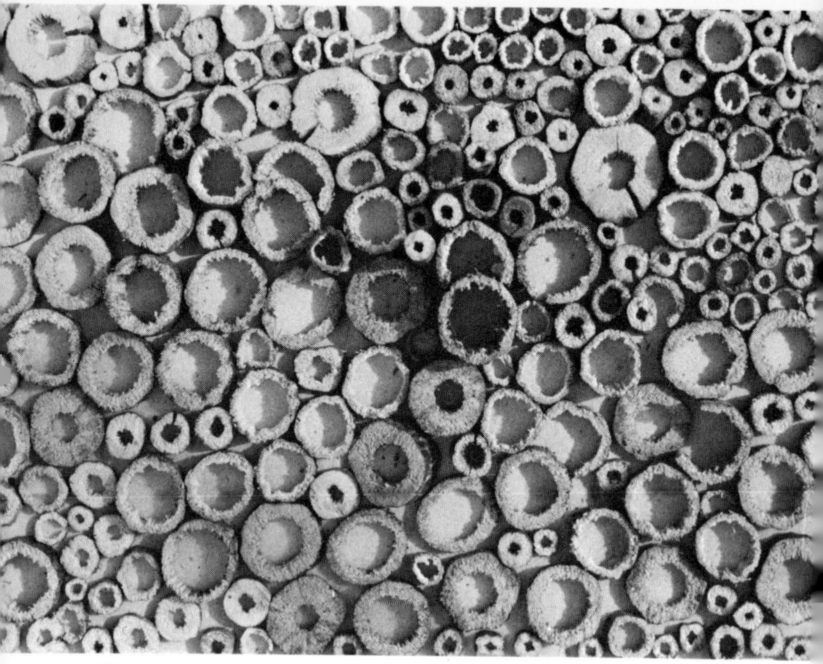

Fig 64

words are they out of harmony with the rest? Perhaps the pattern of the background shapes which you can see between the pieces is not visually satisfying. Did you consider them?

All the above considerations are concerned with the abstract qualities inherent in the exercise. As soon as you become conscious of them it means you are becoming increasingly sensitive to them. This will make all your work more expressive, no matter what your style of painting.

We had a vigorous crop of sunflowers in the garden. At the end of the season the thick stems lay waiting for disposal. I began to saw them up. I became fascinated by the variety of cross-sections. I cut a few dozen about half an inch long. I arranged them on a piece of plywood and glued them on with Bostik (Elmer's glue or Sobo would be the equivalent in U.S.). After some hesitation I painted it white. I then wished I had not done so. The natural colours were much more attractive than the uniform white.

Find some hollow stems and try this exercise. If you have no sunflowers, try bamboo or any other hollow stem – cardboard tubes, old hose pipes, plumbers left-overs, washers, rings. . . .

Motifs from impressing

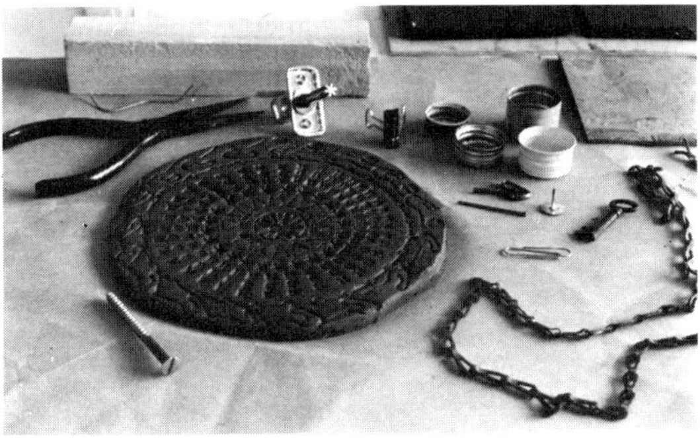

Fig 65 Impressions in clay tile

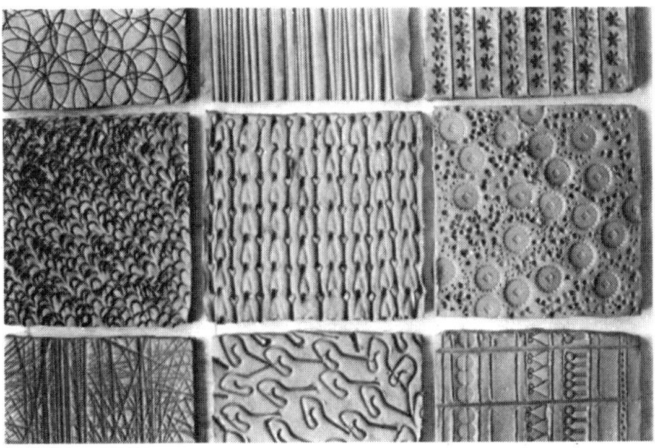

Fig 66 Set of tiles

It is highly likely that you have some clay in your garden. Dig out a spadeful. Take out the bits of grit. Make it into a ball and roll it out to about half an inch thick. From this make a neat tile.

If you cannot find any clay in your garden, or if you don't have a garden, buy a bag from an art shop (*not* plasticine).

Next search round for any object which will make a characterful impression in the clay. Experiment to see what sort of texture pattern you can imprint on the clay. All the textures illustrated in figs 65 and 66 were produced by the objects you can see in fig. 65.

Make a set of tiles and assemble them to make a ceramic panel. This sort of exercise will stimulate that sense of texture which every artist *must* possess.

Motifs from collecting

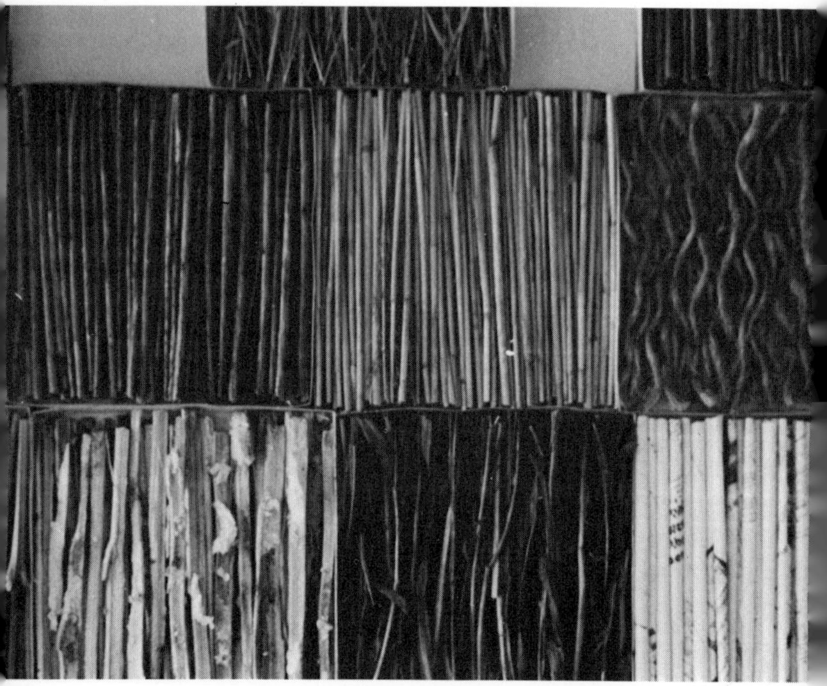

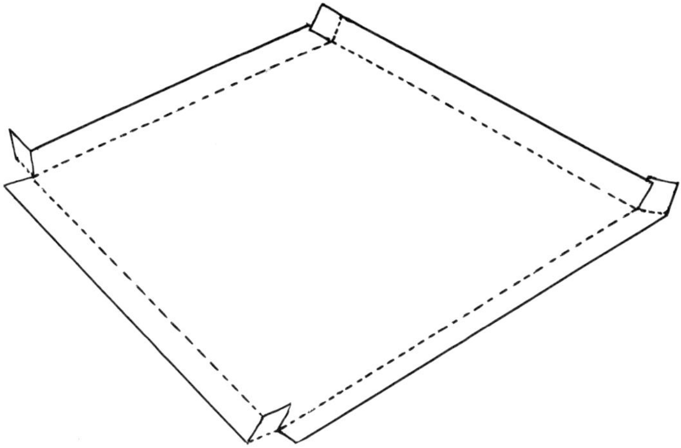

Fig 68 Make trays by folding along all dotted lines, as shown above, and then gluing the corner overlaps

Fig 67 (*opposite*) Trays of textures

One grass stem, by itself, is a grass stem; but make a six-inch-square, shallow, paper tray and fill it with grass stems, and the effect is one of rich texture. Can you identify what is in the other trays of textures in the illustration above? See the solutions on page 103.

It is possible to carry out a fascinating and creative exercise, at minimal cost, which will greatly stimulate your sensitivity to textures, and will occupy you pleasurably for some days.

Look at the diagram in fig. 68. Make a number of these shallow trays. Then systematically collect enough material to fill them all, as in fig. 67 on the previous page. Be very strict with yourself and very disciplined. Let them all be *linear* textures, as in fig. 67, for the first exercise.

As soon as you begin to think in linear terms, ideas will start to occur to you, and before you know where you are, the trays will be full. This is imaginative, conceptual, mental activity. This is *you*, working in an aesthetic, an abstract aesthetic, way. Fig. 69 shows a texture panel in my hall at home. It consists of fifteen seven-inch-square trays filled with textures glued into place, and the trays assembled on, and glued to, a board 44 in. × 22 in. Fig. 70 shows the same panel treated with white paint from an aerosol spray and hanging against a white wall: the effect is subtle and provides a lively talking point when visitors call.

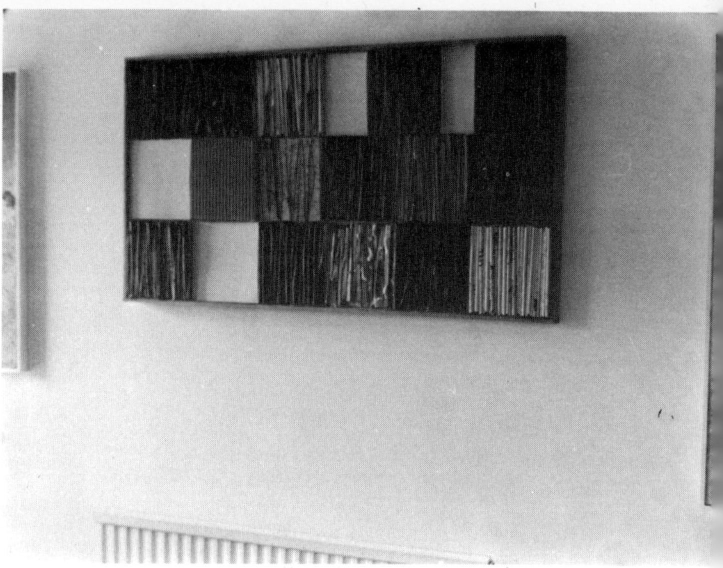

Fig 69

Figs 69–70 Two photographs of the texture-trays panel in situ. Fig. 69 is the natural-coloured panel, fig. 70 the whitened panel

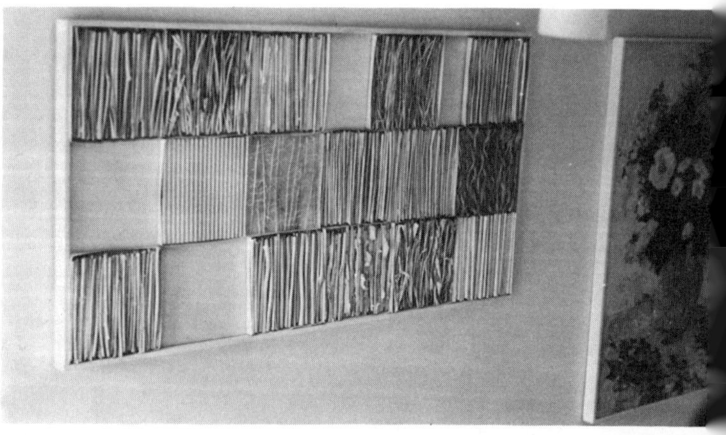

Repeat the project with granular textures – seeds, particles, grains, powders, crumbs, filings, sawdust, scraps, shreds, splinters, fibres, snippets, chips, clippings, shavings, pellets. Explore natural and man-made modules – rice, lentils, buds, leaves, pebbles . . . the list is never-ending.

Visual exploration

The reader will be aware by now that a main aim of this book is to stimulate visual curiosity. Everything I have so far written about, or illustrated, has been concerned with visual exploration – looking, seeing, finding; prizing out the inner secrets of natural forms; modifying, watching, comparing, analyzing, extracting, enlarging, collecting, distorting, manipulating, assembling, arranging, choosing, placing, selecting, isolating, focusing, dissecting.

Every word in this list is meaningful. Every one describes a creative activity which we have already employed in order to examine, in one way or another, our environment. By environment I mean not just the house we live in, the street, the town or landscape, but the *total* environment and every single item in it, including ourselves.

The exploring processes we have already outlined can be applied to every aspect of our environment. Every exploration, in whatever sphere, reveals new and unexpected subject matter. More than this, it provides delight and new awareness of one's world. It takes the scales from one's eyes. The world becomes a richer place. The artist becomes a richer person.

This is perhaps the appropriate point to repeat that visual exploration is relevant to every form of artistic expression, in every medium. In other words, if the artist renders himself visually sensitive and aware, he will have enough ideas and subject-matter, enough visual excitement and delight, to provide stimulus for work in any medium – whether it be painting, which is our main concern, or print-making, batik, sculpture, engraving, modelling, design, or graphic design. It provides food for all these activities; and it doesn't stop there. It flows over to inform the thinking and sensitivities of the photographer, the interior-decorator, the window-dresser, the stage-designer, the dress-designer. . . .

Perhaps it would be more true to say of this book that it is an 'Indirect' how-to-do-it.

All the same, there is a place for explaining certain techniques which produce pictures. Some of these will be dealt with later on. For the moment let us continue by examining one or two more ways of visually exploring the environment.

Study fig. 71. This is a photograph of an image projected onto the studio wall by a domestic slide-projector. It is not a photographic image, but one made by sandwiching a natural form in a plain glass slide.

Motifs from projecting

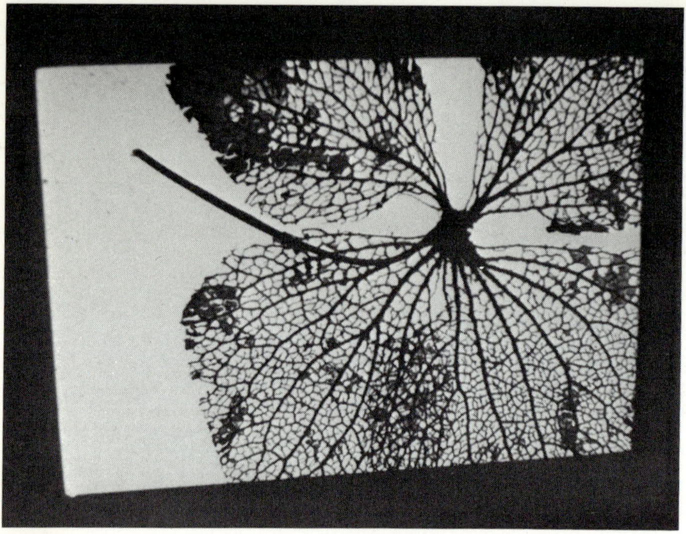

Fig 71 Photograph of projection of slide on screen

Plain, empty, glass slide cases can be bought for about sixpence each (a few cents). They consist, fig. 72, of two thin plates of removable glass in a plastic frame suitable in size for a home projector. Any number of man-made and natural forms can be sandwiched between the two glasses and then projected in the same way as a photographic slide. The image in fig. 71 is of a skeletal hydrangea floweret.

A much cheaper method of making 'sandwich' slides is to use un-needed slide frames from unsuccessful colour transparencies. Stick a layer of Sellotape over one face, then add bits of transparent coloured papers and tintings with inks (felt-tipped pens

Fig 72

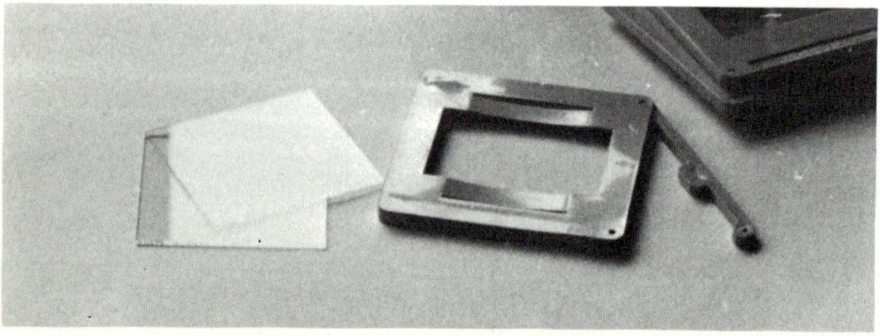

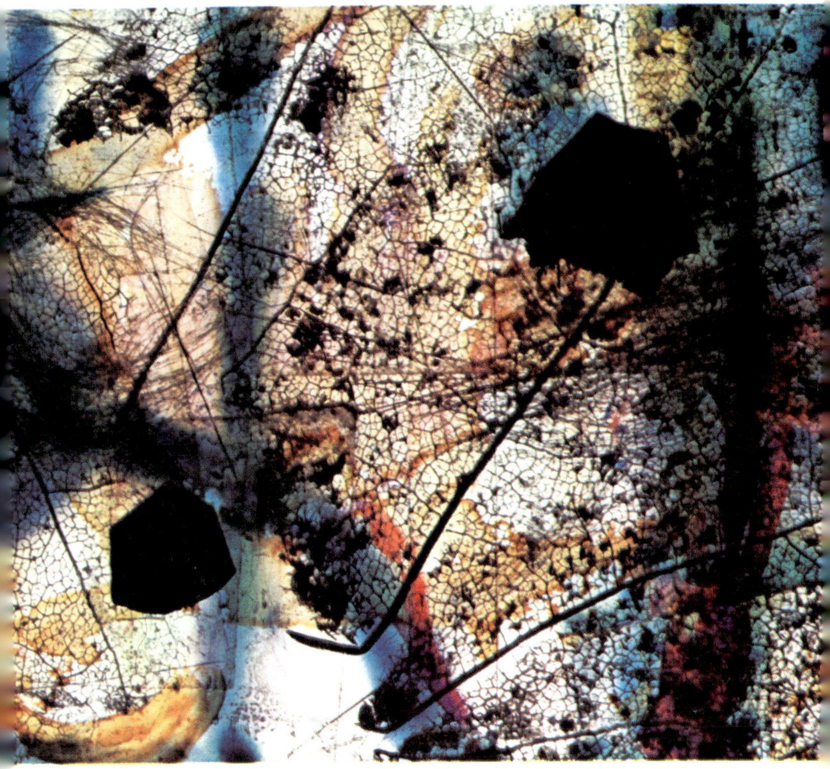

Fig 73 'Home-made' colour slide

work well). Experiment with liquid colours in semi-opaque and opaque forms. To complete the slide, stick a retaining layer of Sellotape on the other face of the slide. Project it. Add to it by referring to what appears on the screen. Alter it, modify it.

The colour abstract in fig. 73 is made from a home-made 'sandwich' slide.

The projected image has great impact. It has the power to focus one's looking. It eliminates extraneous influences. Because of this it enables you to see, to select, to contemplate and to manipulate motifs which you might ultimately use for abstract paintings. Try making a few slides. If you don't have any old slide-cases, cut some out of thin cardboard.

Motifs from printing

Fig 74

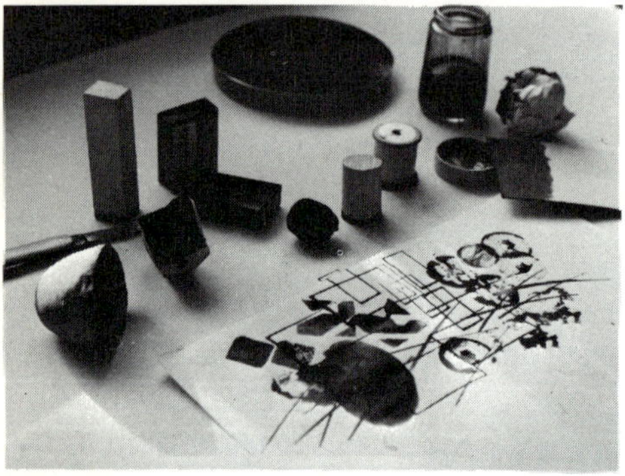

Fig 75

The design illustrated above is a very simple print. The larger shapes were made by crumpling a piece of stiff paper to make a ball, about as big as a golf ball, dipping this into ordinary black ink about quarter of an inch deep in a flat dish or tin lid, and then printing with it. The small round marks were made with the unsharpened end of a pencil, dipped in the same ink.

Scan the surface of this illustration through one of your view-finders; then try another with a different-sized hole. Picture in your mind's eye the design you can see through your view-finder carried out in another colour. Make some prints yourself. Try different colours. You can print with paint or domestic dye. Think up different things to print with – corks, cotton reels (thread spools), small blocks of wood, match-boxes, folded cardboard, potato blocks (potato cuts). . . .

Try enlarging your designs and turning them into paintings. See pages 56–7 for a method of enlarging.

Motifs from rubbings

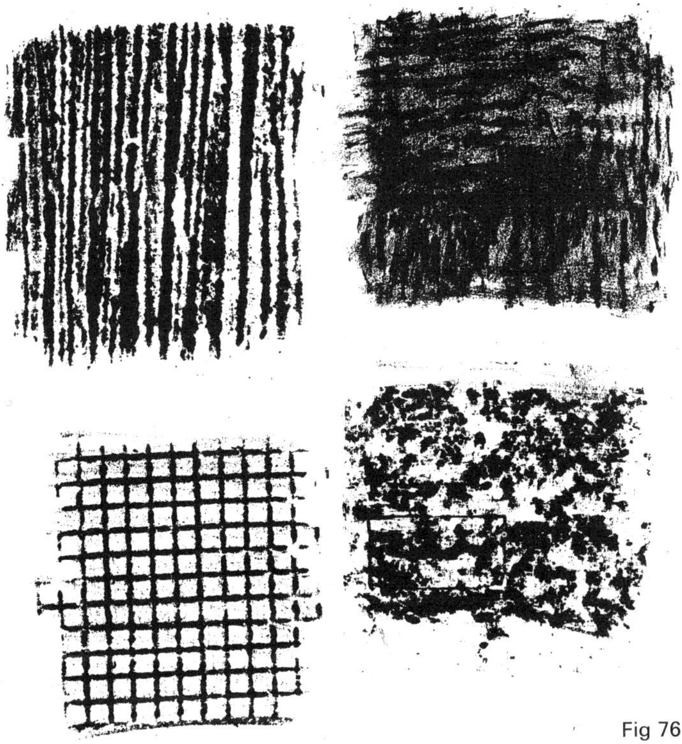

Fig 76

The designs on this page were produced by rubbing. Take a thick black grease crayon, or a soft pencil, and a sheet of thin paper. Place the paper over any interestingly-textured surface you can find, and rub the crayon over an area of the paper, taking care not to miss any. The pattern of the surface underneath will appear on the paper. In fig. 76 the top left rubbing is from a glass door, top right from a rush mat, bottom left from an electric fire and bottom right from a house brick.

Whether or not your design is interesting will depend on how curiously and painstakingly you search, how imaginatively you look, how creatively you think.

Once again scan the surface and see if any motif presents itself for work on a larger scale.

N.B. grease crayon is the best to use. It is quickest and most effective.

Enlarging by squaring-up

The motif in fig. 77 is from one of the rubbings in fig. 76. Can you spot it? I think it would look interesting on a larger scale. If you wish to enlarge a motif and retain the character of the design, you can do this by squaring-up. This is basically a system of increasing all the dimensions but keeping the proportions constant. For instance a design 3 ft × 1 ft is 144 times larger in area than one 3 in. × 1 in., but the proportion is the same.

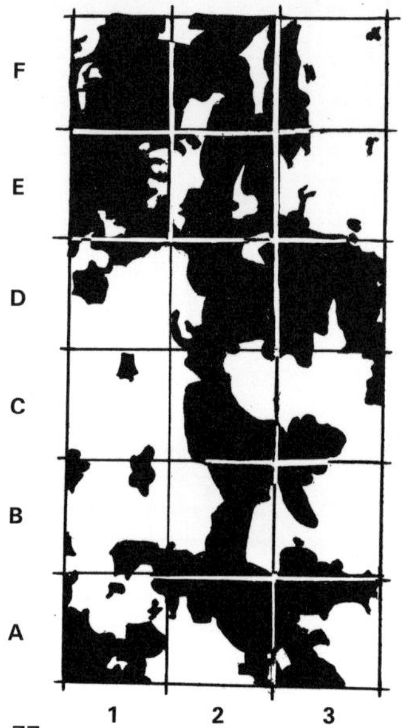

Fig 77

Look at fig. 77. The long sides are cut into 6 divisions, and the short sides into 3 divisions, of equal length. This makes 18 squares. Fig. 78 is a larger rectangle. That also is divided into 6×3 equal divisions, giving 18 squares. Look carefully at square A.1. in the small grid. Repeat that portion of the design contained in it, exactly, in A.1. in the large grid. Repeat for A.2. Continue all over the large grid, and the enlarged design will grow into place.

I have left about half for you to finish. When you have completed it, find a 3 in. × 1½ in. motif of your own and enlarge that to, say, 2 ft × 4 ft. Decorators' lining paper is very good for this kind of experimental work. A good-sized roll is quite inexpensive.

Another example of the use of squaring-up will be found on pages 84–5.

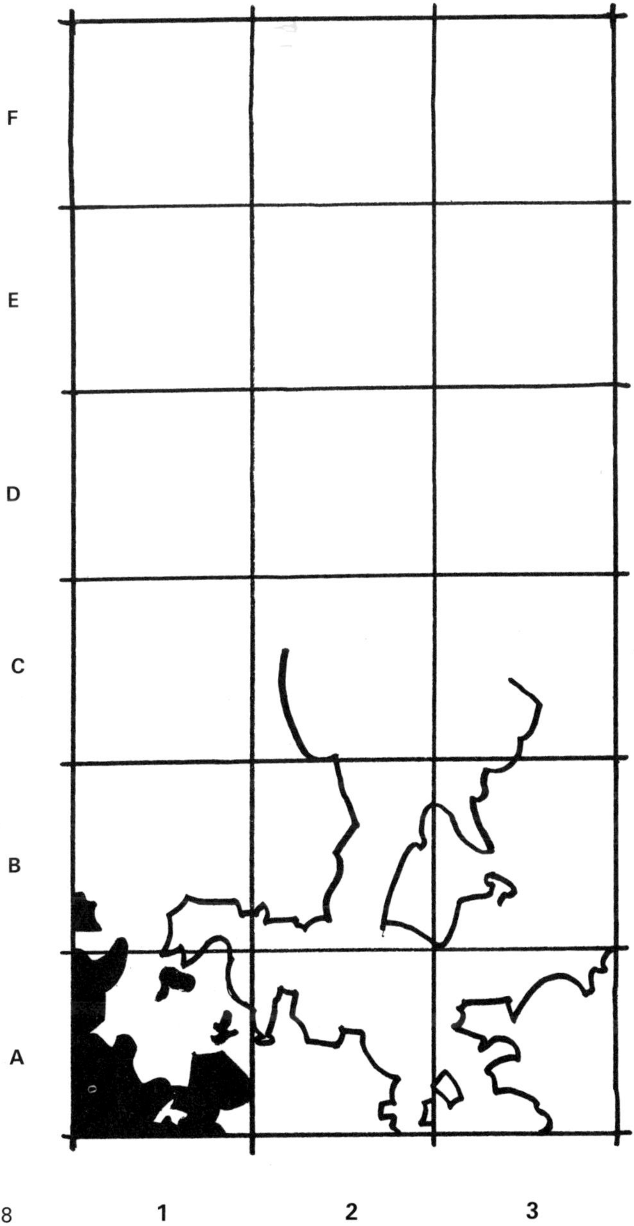

Fig 78

Motifs from doodles

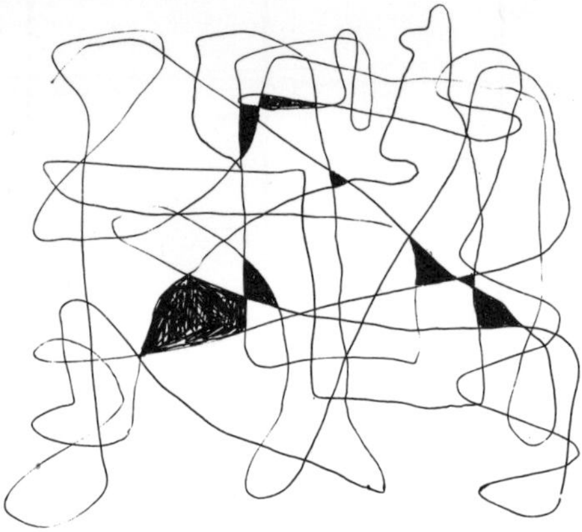

Fig 79

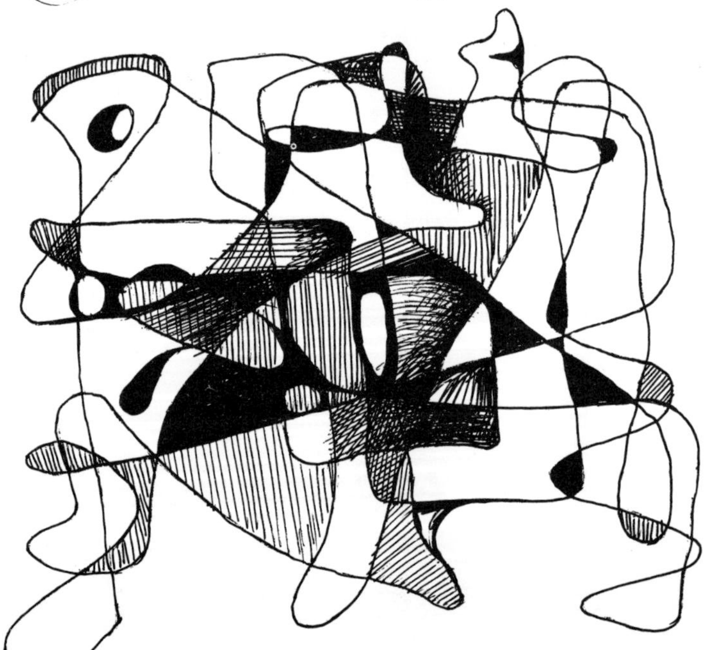

Fig 80 Developed doodle

The Oxford Dictionary defines the word doodle as 'an aimless scrawl while one's attention is engaged elsewhere'.

We have all seen doodles in telephone booths, on the margins of school-books and, indeed, sprinkled pretty well all round our environment. We have all made our own doodles from time to time. Some doodles are highly intricate and complex drawings, to which the word scrawl can hardly apply. In fact one wonders whether the Oxford definition is somewhat superficial.

I believe a subconscious aesthetic takes over when doodling starts. Doodling is automatic drawing, sensitive, and generally stemming from abstract stimuli. Many contemporary artists use this approach. It is a valuable exercise to sit down with a ball-point pen and a plain postcard and deliberately produce a doodle. Try it! Start by putting the pen to the paper. Make any mark at random. Then look at what you have done and see whether you get a 'feeling' about where the next mark should go. As this book is about abstract art, let it be an abstract doodle. Keep the 'bug-eyed monsters' out of it, and restrict yourself to pattern, line, outline-shape, filled-in-shape, texture, tone. Let the developing design control you. Let it suggest to you what you should put next and where you should put it. Don't add anything until you feel compelled to. If nothing comes, don't force it, and don't be disappointed. Stop, and try again some other day. It *will* work, sooner or later.

The design on the previous page, fig. 79, was made in this way. I took a tracing from it, so that I could do some more work on it and still preserve the original, so as to be able to compare the two. Which version do you prefer? Fig. 79 or fig. 80?

At any rate, this kind of automatic-doodle drawing is a way of generating and developing graphic ideas. It is a generating process, as distinct from an extracting process, or an analytical process.

You are interested in abstract expression. This is a method you must explore.

Drips, blots, splashes

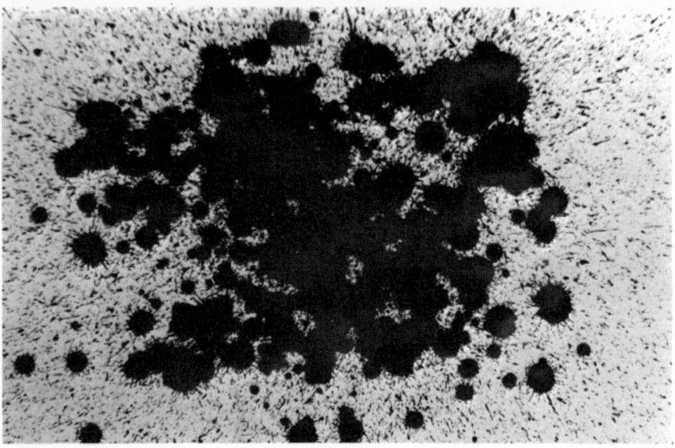

Fig 81

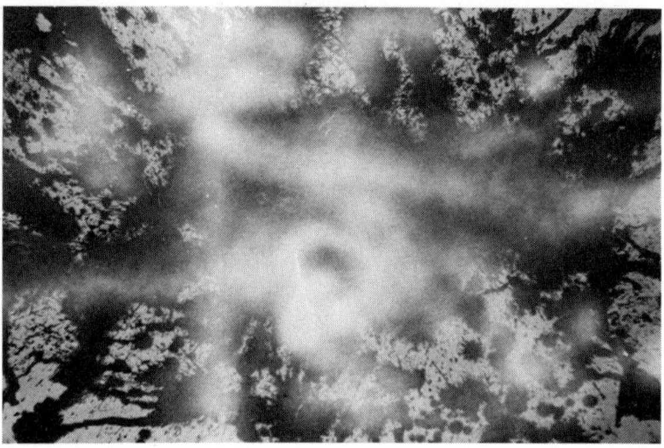

Fig 82

The brush as the artist's main tool was predominant for at least five centuries, until the beginning of the twentieth century in fact. Yet there is no logical reason why the brush should have had the monopoly for so long. The use of the palette knife as a layer-on-of-paint was a step away from tradition. Then Braque and his circle began to experiment with new ways of making pictures – using a sharp point to draw through the paint film, gluing prefabricated shapes to canvas or board, carving images in low relief in various materials. It was a short step from inventing new ways of presenting old motifs to thinking of using these new ways to present *new* motifs. So we arrive at the point when the Abstract Expressionists, the so-called Action Painters, say 'it doesn't matter how you get the motif onto the canvas or paper, so long as you get what you want where you want it! This is

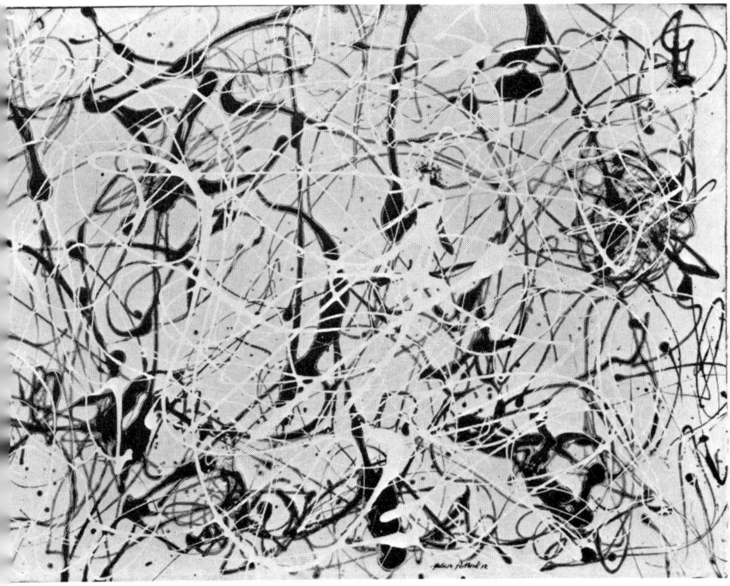

Fig 83 *Number 23* by Jackson Pollock 1948. Tate Gallery, London

logical. So why not throw the colour on from a distance, or ride bicycles with inky tyres across the canvas, if the treads of the tyres print the sort of pattern you want. Who hasn't had his eye caught by a car-print in the snow, or wet shoe-sole print on a nice dry floor? I remember watching a television programme which showed an artist at work. His nude female model was coated with paint and she pressed parts of her body against the canvas, as directed by the artist, and left her print behind. Jackson Pollack laid his canvas on the floor and dripped paint onto it from, amongst other things, a tin can with a perforated bottom. Fig. 81 was produced by laying a piece of paper on the ground and allowing ink squeezed from a sponge to fall on it. Fig. 82 was made by numerous shots from a toy-water-pistol charged with ink, the result subsequently overlaid by areas of paint sprayed from an aerosol (spray can). In both cases, the technique was repeated many times and the best motif was selected. This method of working is not to be dismissed as a crazy activity. It is the calculated use of accidental effect; and the exercise of firm discrimination in choosing only those motifs suitable for development. Try it yourself. If you cannot borrow a water-pistol, detergent containers, with nozzles, will do just as well.

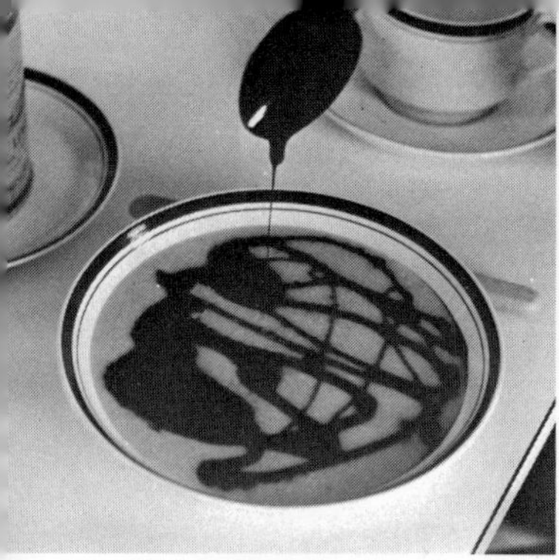

Fig 84 Black treacle on porridge

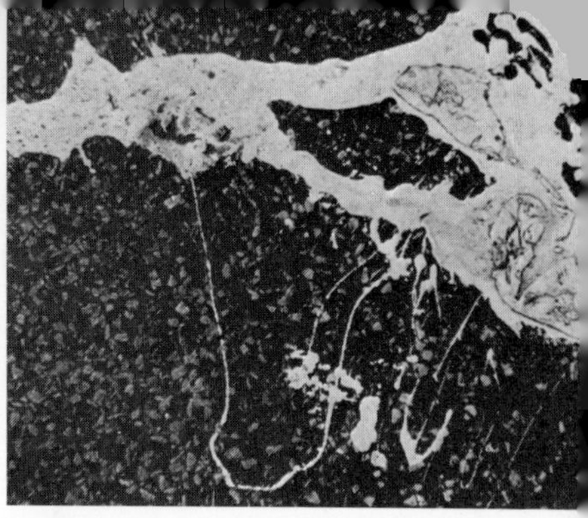

Fig 85 Spilt paint

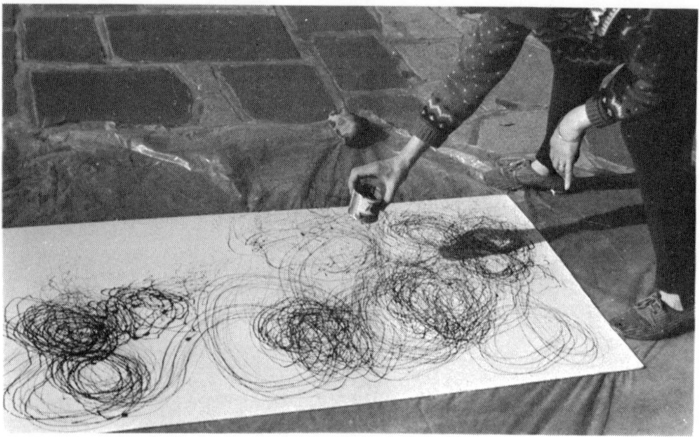

Fig 86 An enthusiastic amateur artist, aided by a brisk breeze, tries Jackson Pollock's method of dripping paint from a perforated tin-can.

Fig. 87 shows the result. The threads of paint produce an exquisite filigree effect

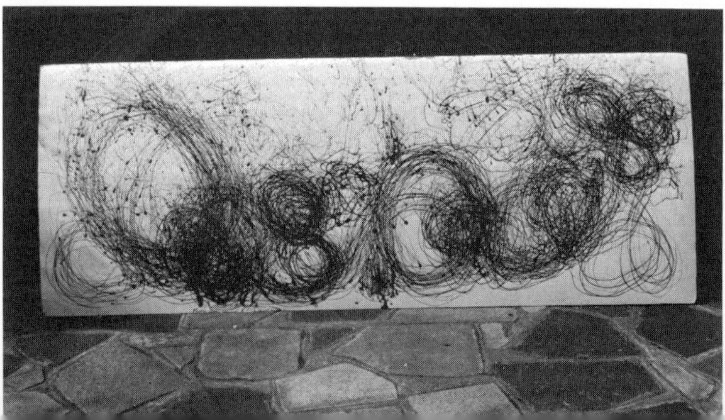

The camera as aid

The sensitive artist is almost bound to be a good photographer. The converse is not so frequently the case. But every dedicated abstract artist will use the camera for all he is worth to collect, find, isolate, procure, keep, and store up visual material for use in future paintings.

The camera is the most flexible and the most powerful aid for the abstract artist. The camera, along with the sketch book, are two indispensable pieces of equipment. If you can afford it, buy a good camera. A single-lens reflex, which enables you to get close up to your subject, is the most useful, but a lot can be done with quite an inexpensive model of standard design. The valuable features of the camera are that it is selective; that the built-in viewfinder isolates the motif by taking it out of its surroundings; that it has the property of focusing attention on specific components of the environment; that it can provide the artist with permanent records of fugitive (non-permanent) material; and that because it provides a permanent record it makes prolonged, or deferred, study possible. The effect of light shown in the illustration on page 31 (fig. 42) lasted about ninety seconds.

The camera and the computer share some characteristics. The computer is only a machine, but, programmed correctly, it will work miracles. Aim the camera at the right things and it will do the same. The good photograph is the product of visual sensitivity, a sense of composition, a knowledge of abstract values, a feeling for scale, and a response to balance and harmony.

Most of this book is devoted to the finding, extracting, making of subject matter for art work. In my view every means is legitimate, including the use of optical aids which are, after all, a means of extending the seeing-power of the human eye.

The magnifying-glass is another invaluable accessory. I always keep one in my pocket. Many subtle textures and other unexpected features are revealed by its use. Without it they might have gone un-noticed.

The microscope can open up a world invisible to the naked eye and reveal rare, strange and magical visual images which will set the creative mind working. Fig. 93 shows a cross-section of pine root, fig. 94 is the head and thorax of an ant.

The illustrations on pages 64–5 show the sort of motifs the camera can find when it is coupled to an inquisitive human eye.

Fig 88 Snow and grass texture

Fig 89 Lobster in Dieppe fishmonger's tank

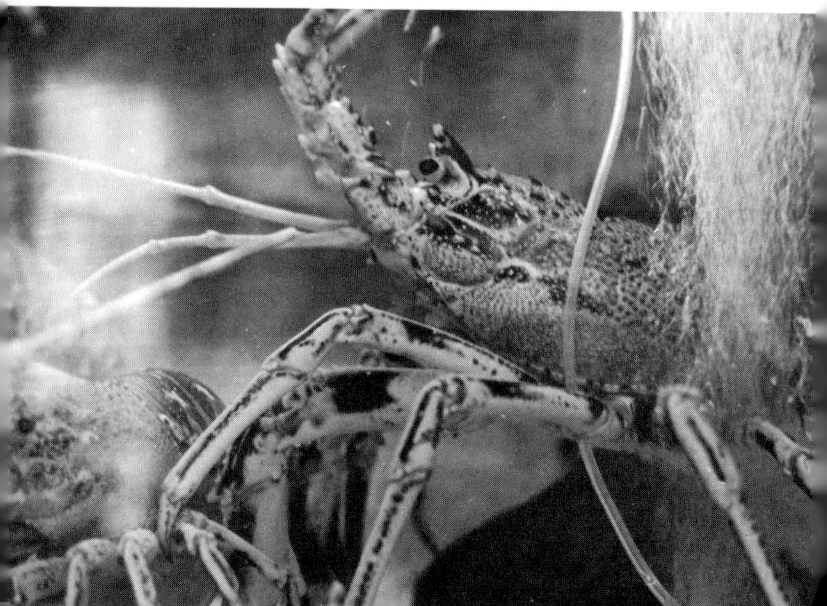

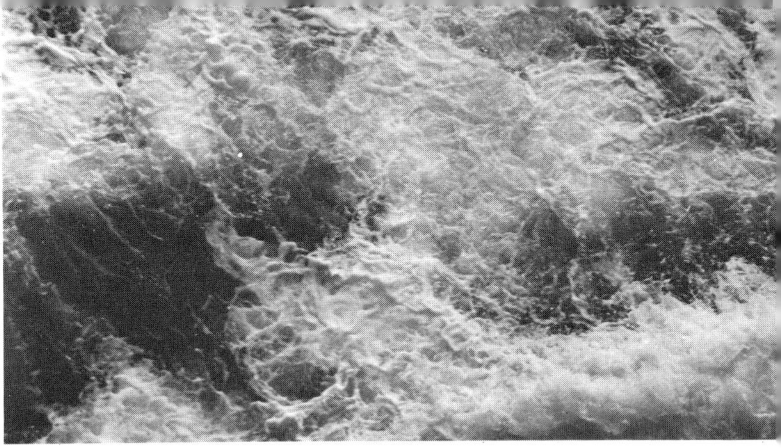

Fig 90 Bow wave of Cross Channel Ferry

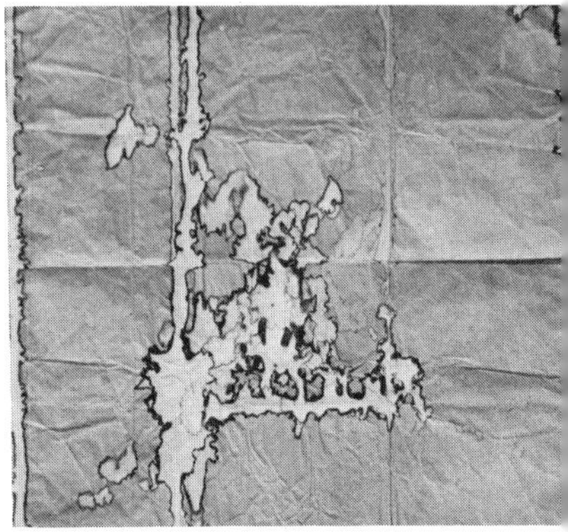

Fig 91 Damp stain on a wall in Paris

Fig 92 Close-up of elephant hide

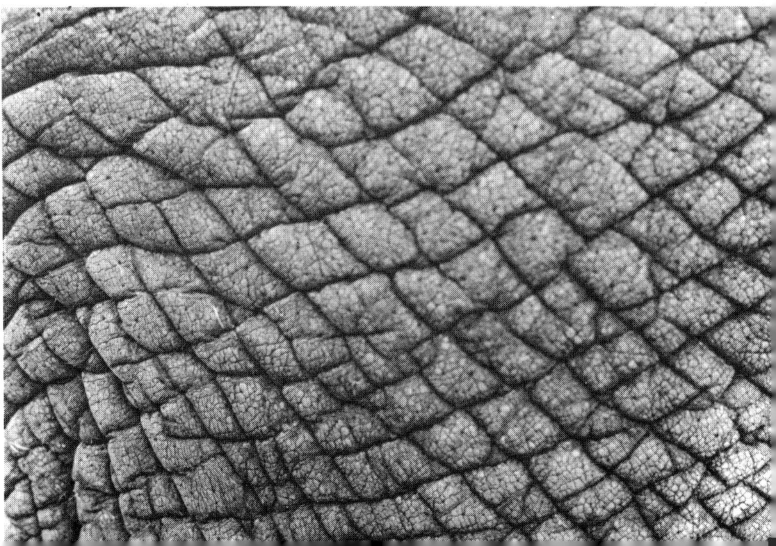

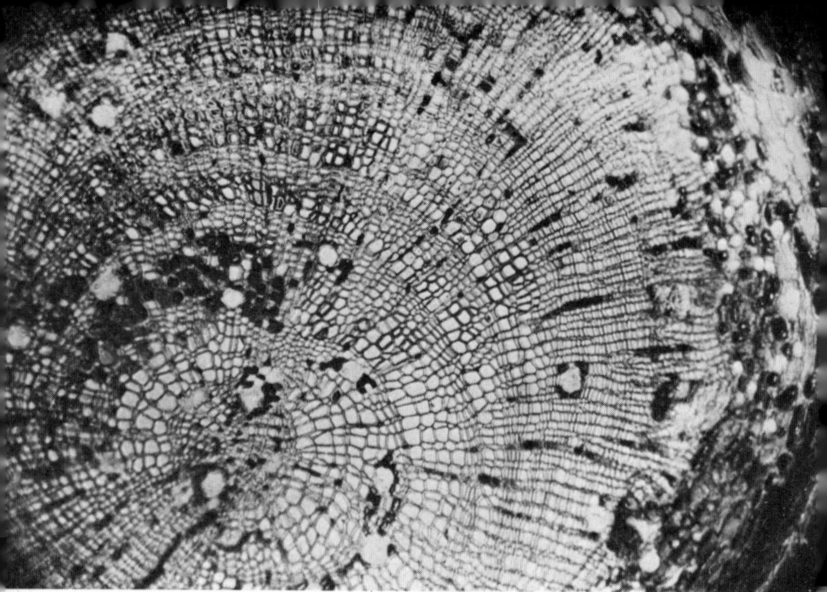

Fig 93

Fig 94

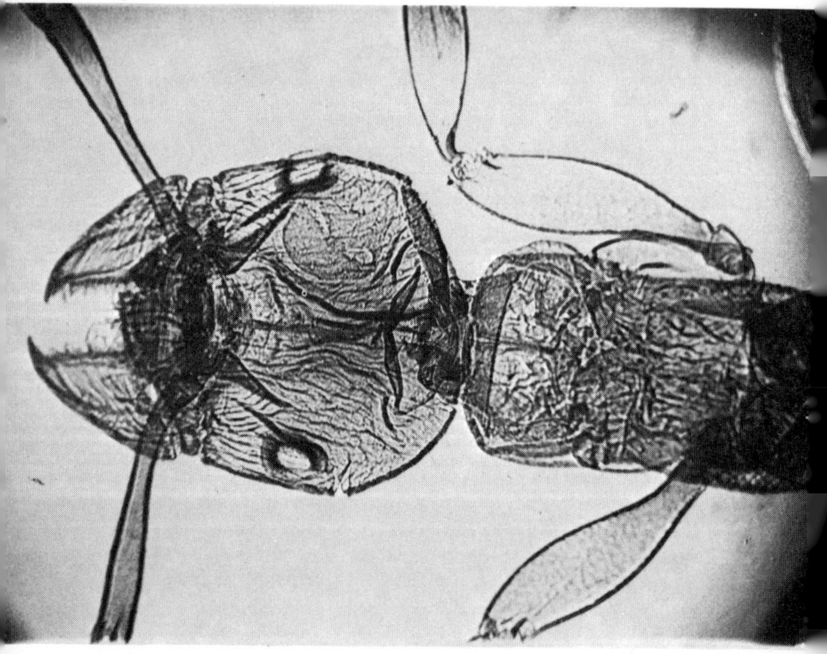

Found abstract

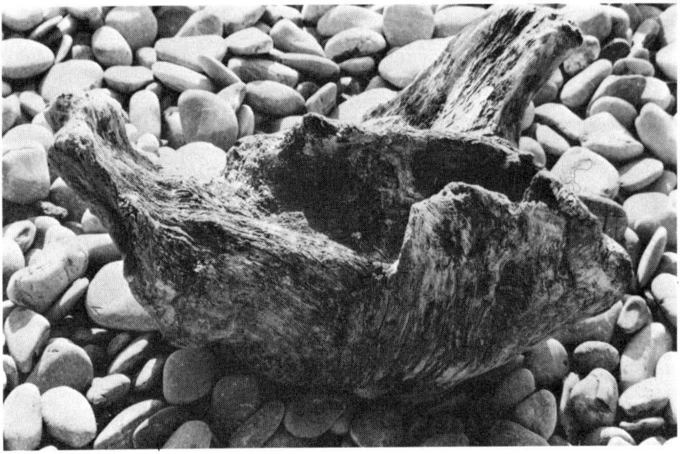

Fig 95

When an artist is engaged in producing a work of art, he is concerned with imposing his will upon materials of various kinds – stone, wood, clay, paint, cloth, metal. In every case he achieves his aim by making shapes of, or with, his chosen material.

The artefact he produces consists of a material which has been shaped by the artist to the dictates of his creative imagination. It is a material of some kind which has been rendered into a form – embroidery, painting, sculpture, pottery, and so on. In order that the form may be realized, in one of the above media, there must be an intermediate agency, i.e. man, the artist. If the form he makes is attractive, gives pleasure, and conforms to accepted standards, it is said to be beautiful.

Is man an indispensable agent?

It frequently happens that forms are produced by natural forces – erosion, eruption, the action of wind and weather, the activities of organic life, the constant wearing movement of the sea on rock, pebble, driftwood, sea-defences. Without the intervention of man these processes produce, from time to time, forms which by any standard are beautiful and artistic. They are always abstract. The ability to recognize these 'works of art' calls for a refined aesthetic sense. The practice of finding and selecting them, of taking them out of their natural context and making them apparent, is every bit as creative as actually making the forms oneself.

This finding is a form of abstract art. No technical skill is required to 'find'. To practise finding will develop your awareness of pure abstract form.

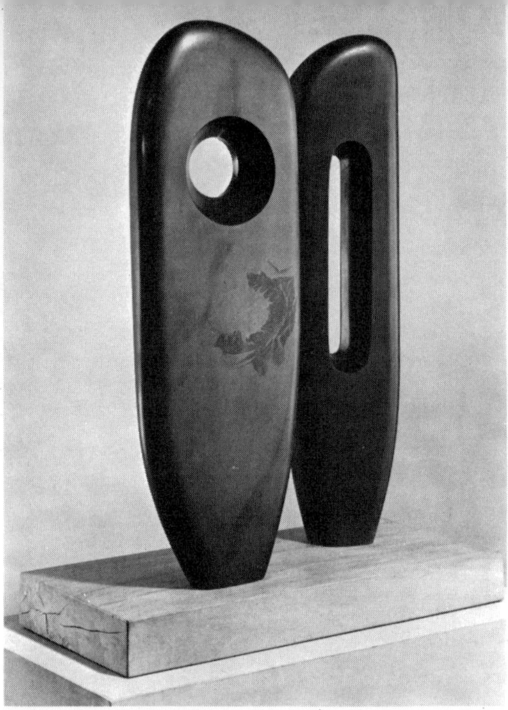

Fig 96

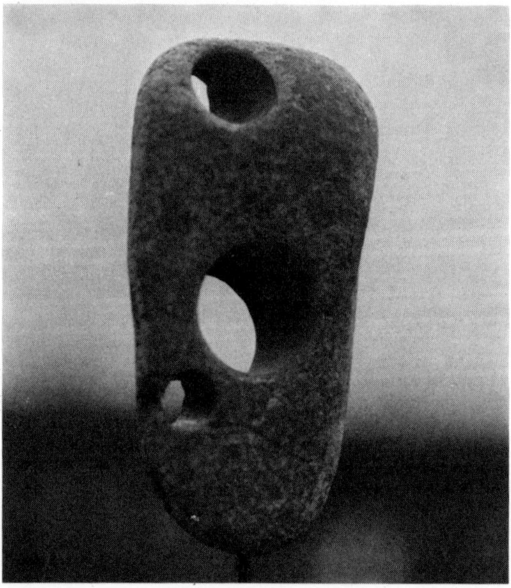

Fig 97

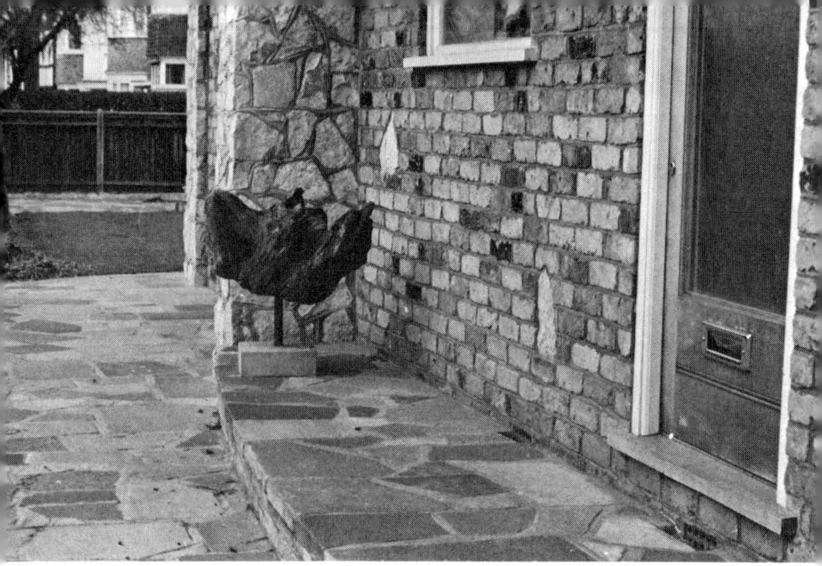

Fig 98

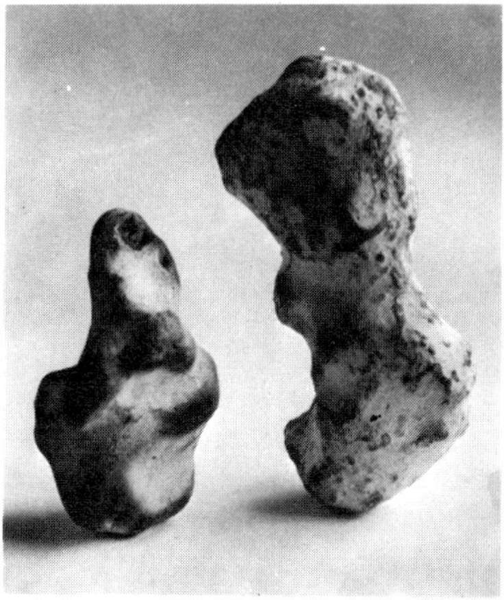

Fig 99

Figs 96 and 97 show two very similar forms, one made by man, one made by the sea.

Is it possible to define the difference between them from the aesthetic point of view? Which is the 'found' form? Which is the 'man-made' form. See the solutions on page 103.

Fig. 98 above shows the large driftwood, seen previously in Fig. 95, mounted on a low plinth and standing by my front doorstep. It attracts attention and comment, and is popular as a swivelling seat with visiting small children.

Fig. 99. Two flints. The larger is a fossilized pelvis, unidentified, but about human size!

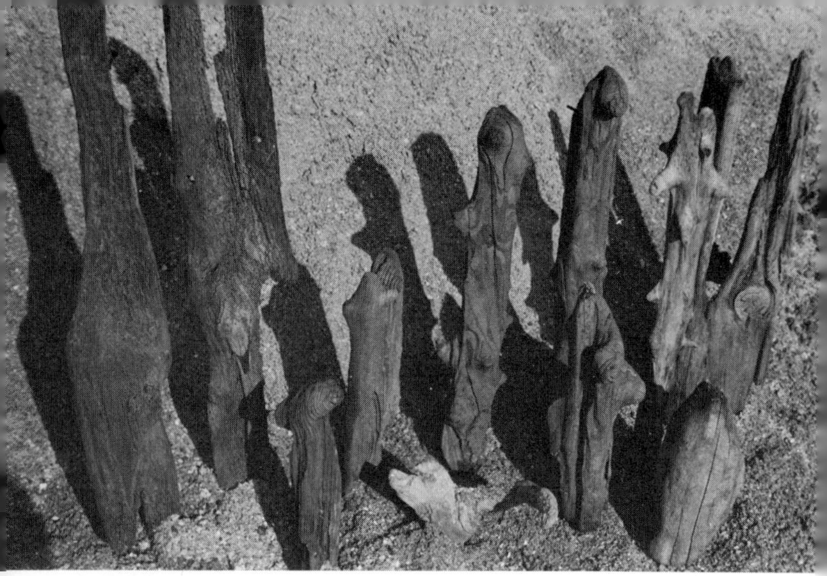

Fig 100

Fig 101

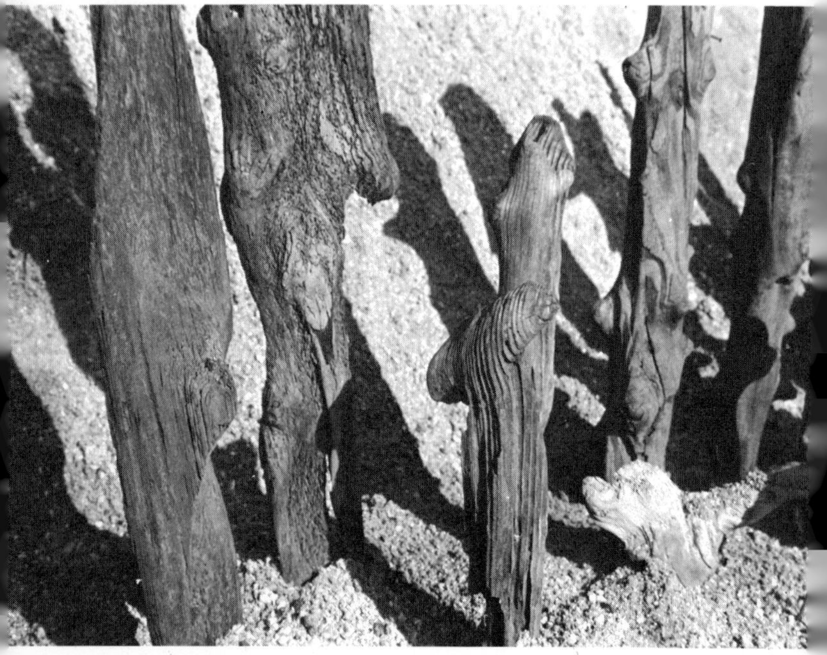

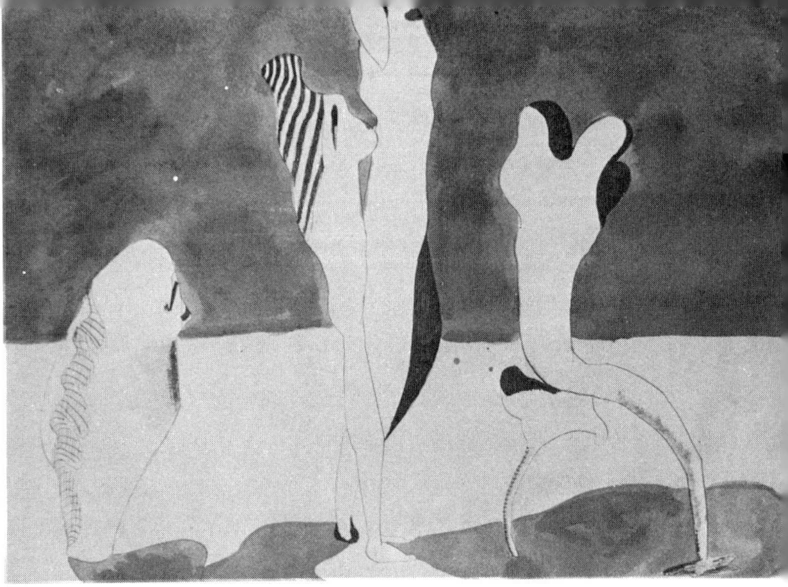

Fig 102

Fig 103

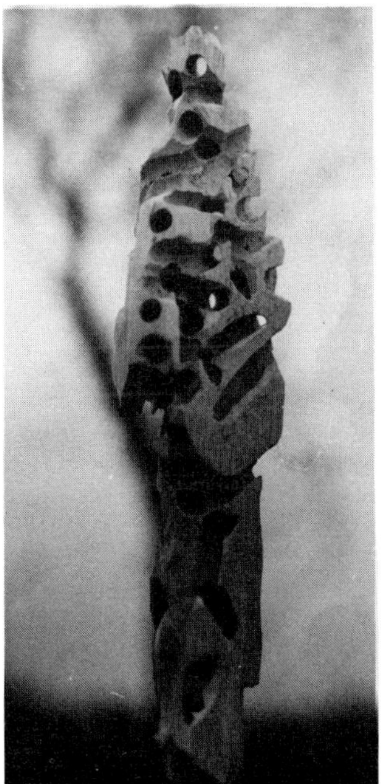

Found-art objects frequently contain within themselves the germs of motifs for work in other media. Fig. 102 is a drawing, by a fifteen-year-old boy, from the grotesques shown in Figs 100–1. These grotesques are all that remain of wooden railway sleepers which were pile-driven into the beach fifty years ago to make breakwaters. The protuberances are knots in the wood, which wore away more slowly than the softer surrounding wood.

Fig. 103 is a piece of drift-wood perforated by boring sea-creatures. The total effect was helped a little by the discreet use of a sharp pocket-knife.

You will have noted that in this section we have considered form as form; and we have avoided incidental likenesses, of stones to buffaloes or twigs to giraffes, etc.

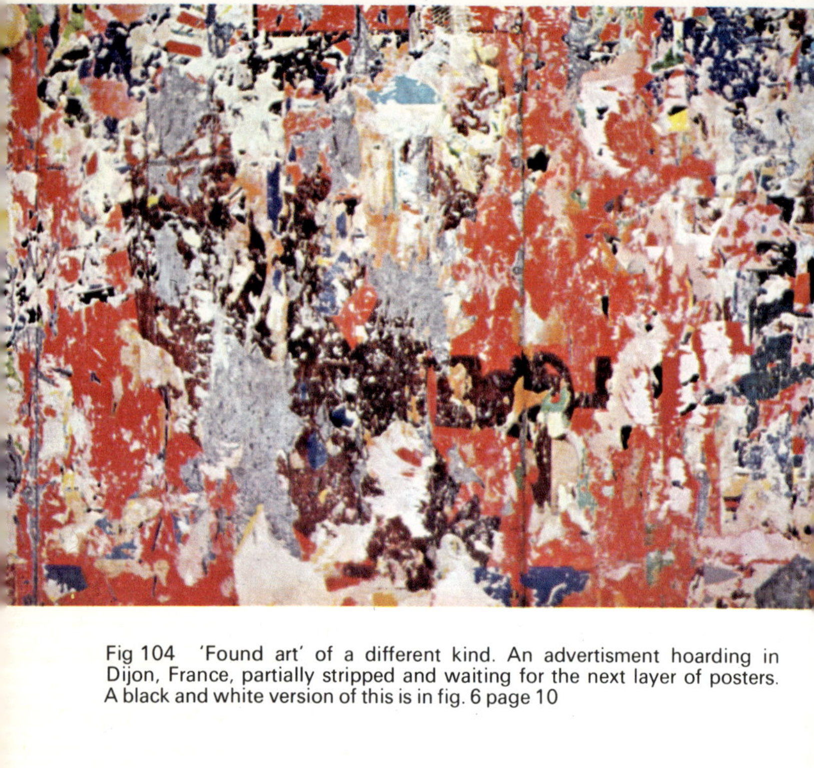

Fig 104 'Found art' of a different kind. An advertisment hoarding in Dijon, France, partially stripped and waiting for the next layer of posters. A black and white version of this is in fig. 6 page 10

Counterchange

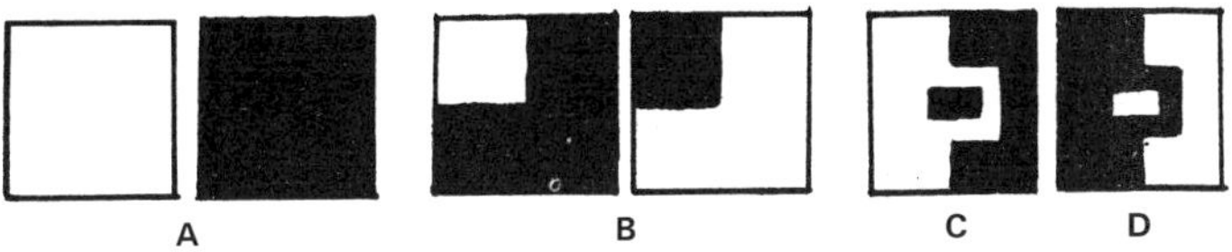

Fig 105 Simple counterchange diagram

Counterchange is a decorative device relying upon pattern, tonal contrast, and the opposition of black to white, dark to light, or at least darker to lighter. Simple examples are a checked gingham dress, a black and white square tiled kitchen floor, or a chess board.

The counterchange of a white square is a black square, fig. 105A. The counterchange of a square with one quarter white and three-quarters black, is a square with one quarter black and three quarters white, fig. 105B. The counterchange of fig. 105C above is fig. 105D. Fig. 106 shows counterchange applied to 'the pebble'.

Counterchange of tone and/or colour can be used in varying degrees of complexity and subtlety in the composition of formal abstract design; or as an abstract, pattern, component of any kind of illustration or picture.

Pattern is our next heading.

Fig 106

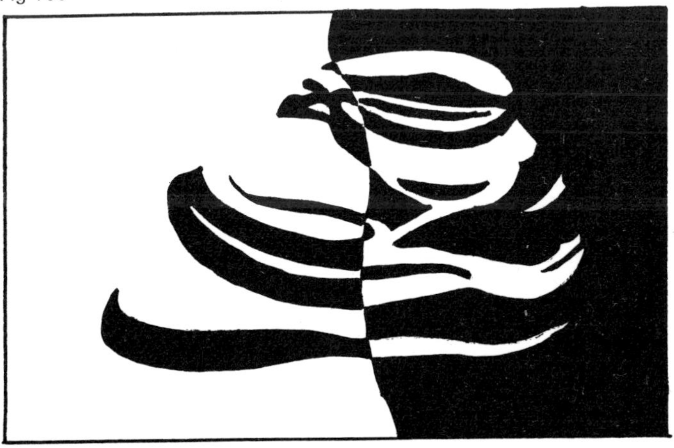

Pattern

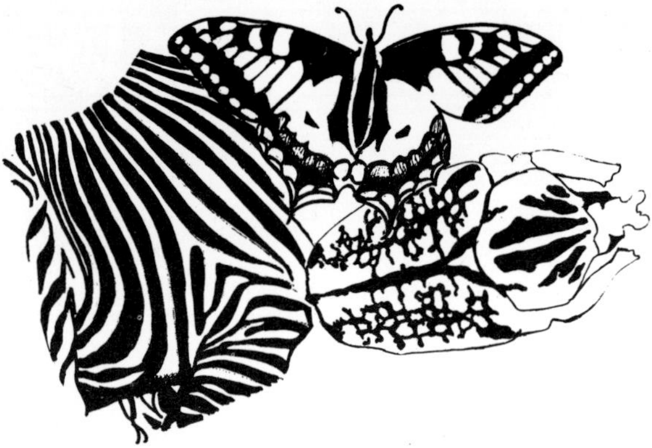

Fig 107

Fig 108

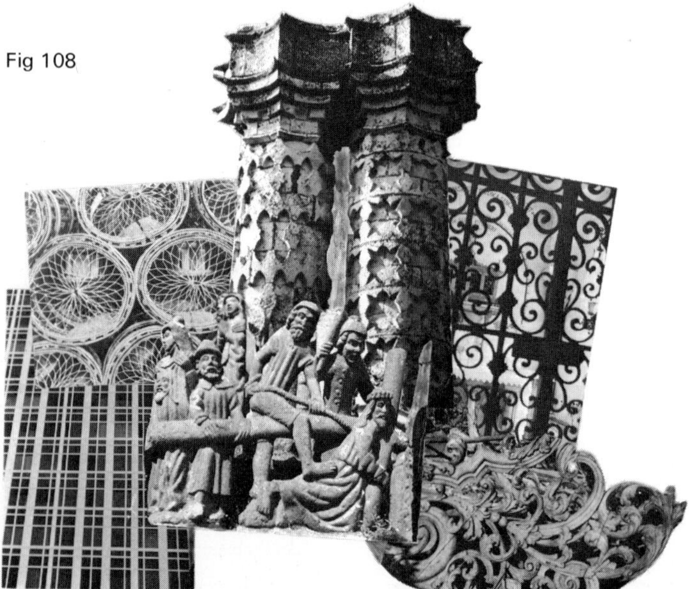

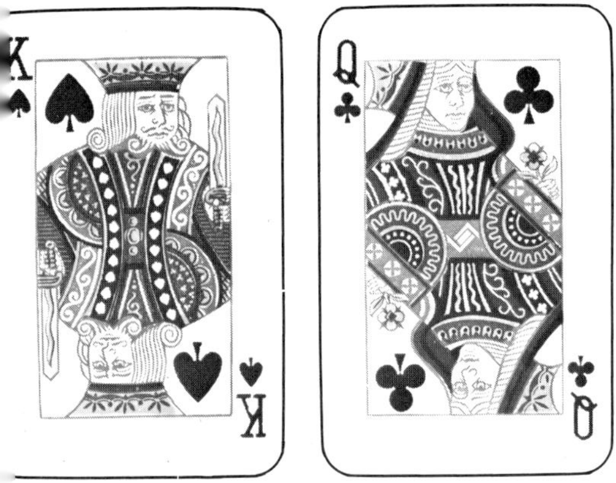

Fig 109

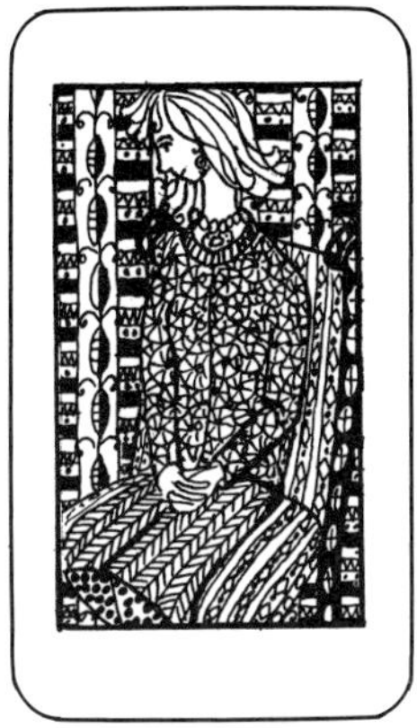

Fig 110

Words are imprecise as a means of communicating visual concepts. The word pattern, for instance, conjures up different mental images to different people. The dressmaker, the boatbuilder, the teacher of young children, the wallpaper manufacturer, the minister of religion all interpret the word differently.

An attempt at definition was made on page 20. This section is intended to reinforce that definition by illustrating three different types of abstract, which, by their nature, are likely to provide you with visual images which you might subsequently use as motifs for art work. Fig 107 is a montage of patterns drawn from the animal world which, it is hoped, will start you looking for other examples. Fig. 108 shows man-made patterns. Take your sketch book or camera and see what you can find. Thirdly, fig. 109 illustrates a familiar form, the playing card – a stylized, conventional design filled out with formal pattern which is completely abstract in kind. Try designing a set of playing cards. Lastly, fig. 110 shows an outline drawing enriched by the addition of abstract pattern. How about making your Christmas Cards next year in this style? Make simple outlines and then fill in the shapes and backgrounds as in figs 109 and 110.

Simplification

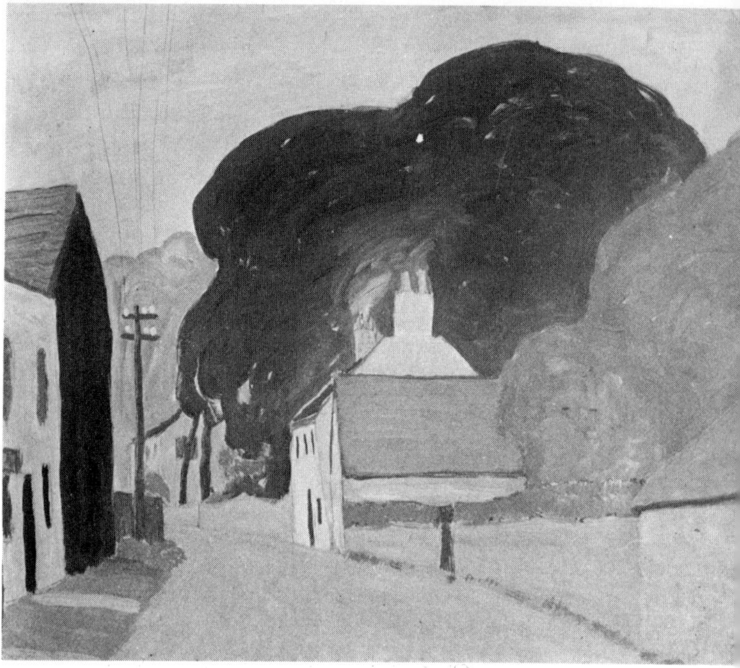

Fig 111

Fig 112 (*opposite*)

How many leaves might there be on a mature elm tree in the height of summer?

The artist would find it impossible, even if he were misguided enough to try, to paint every leaf. What does he do? He looks at the total outline of the green shape made by the mass of leaves and he paints an 'all-over' green shape which corresponds to that mass. Later he may add a texture which suggests leaves, but his first statement will be the large flat shape of green. What he paints will be a simplification of what is before him. Fig. 111 shows a painting by a beginner where all the shapes – road, walls, houses, trees – are simplified.

The degree of simplification determines the degree of abstraction, in this kind of painting. If you simplify everything, severely, you arrive at a state of almost complete abstraction. Fig. 112, *Fields Under Snow*, is an example of extreme simplification. Even the trees were simplified out, in order to underline the feeling of big fields, fresh snow and loneliness. It is a large painting, six feet by four feet.

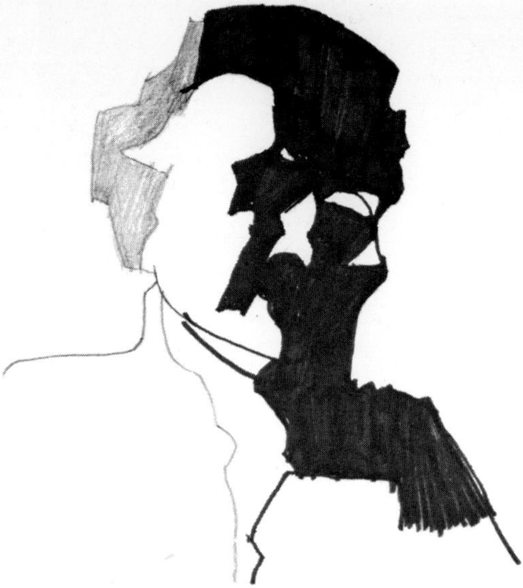

Fig 113 A transcription from Daumier shows how intense lighting and a measure of simplification can reduce a head to two or three abstract shapes representing the dark planes and the light planes. Drawing by non-specialist

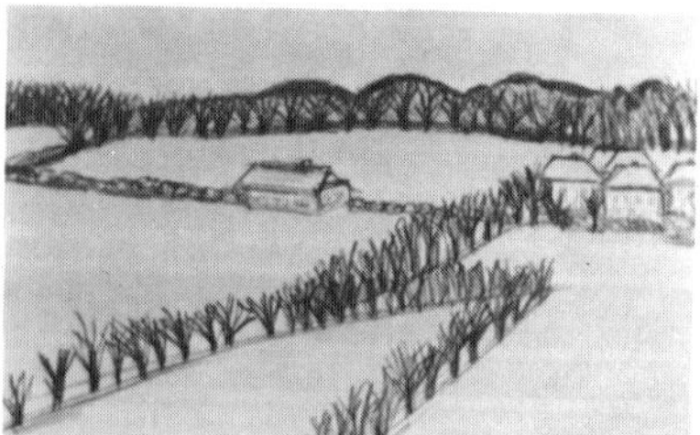

Fig 114 Extreme simplification of tone, plus counterchange. Drawing by non-specialist

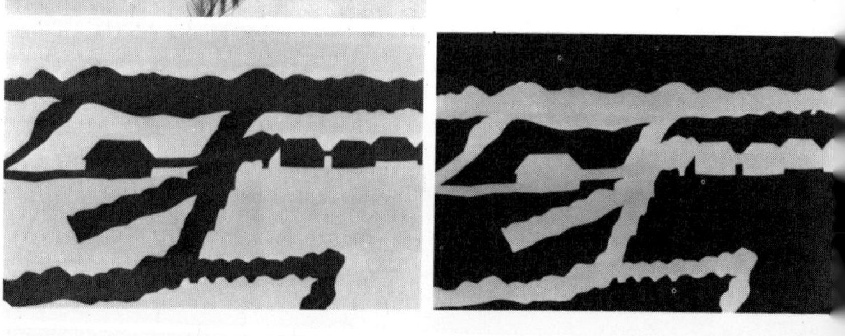

Drawing as abstraction

Some people, it seems, are born with the ability to draw, others struggle all their lives to acquire it. It is my belief that everybody can draw, once they have got rid of outmoded concepts of what drawing is.

For some illogical reason, drawing has become synonymous with 'copying from nature', and the particular aspect of nature most frequently thought of in this context is the nude female figure. This convention is almost entirely a phenomenon of western culture and has been with us for only about five hundred years. Before that this view of drawing did occasionally manifest itself – in, for instance, the Bayeux Tapestry and Gothic manuscripts. Nevertheless the convention has become ingrained, and we have to remind ourselves that drawing the human figure and its anatomy is only a part of the matter. The Greeks in their graphic work, the Egyptians, the Mughals, the Byzantine artists, the Oriental artists practised arts which were rooted in abstract forms.

It is certainly true to say that an awareness of abstract shape and of line is an invaluable aid to drawing of whatever kind. Look at fig. 115. There you will see an assembly of 'shapes of objects' and also of 'shapes of spaces between the objects'. The drawing was made by selecting one shape as a starting point (marked 1) and then adding shapes to it, one by one. I have numbered the sequence to help you to follow the progression of the work.

I have separated out the various shapes and printed them as a row of outlines. When they are looked at out of context, fig. 116, they do not make sense; but, in order to produce this drawing, those abstract shapes had to be seen, selected and drawn. When they are assembled together they are still basically abstract; they are still the same shapes, but now they are significant because they are related one to another. The sum of the whole is greater than the sum of the parts.

I urge you to practise this method of drawing. Draw the 'between' shapes. See them as abstract shapes. Place them in your composition as abstract shapes. (This thesis of drawing is dealt with fully in *You Can Draw* in the same series as this book.)

Always carry a small sketchbook. Wherever and whenever possible make notes, or detailed sketches, of motifs and ideas. Make a collection and save every bit of interesting visual information about likely abstract subject matter. Store it up in your sketchbook. Back at home, who knows what may 'spark off' as you sit at your ease and turn the pages again.

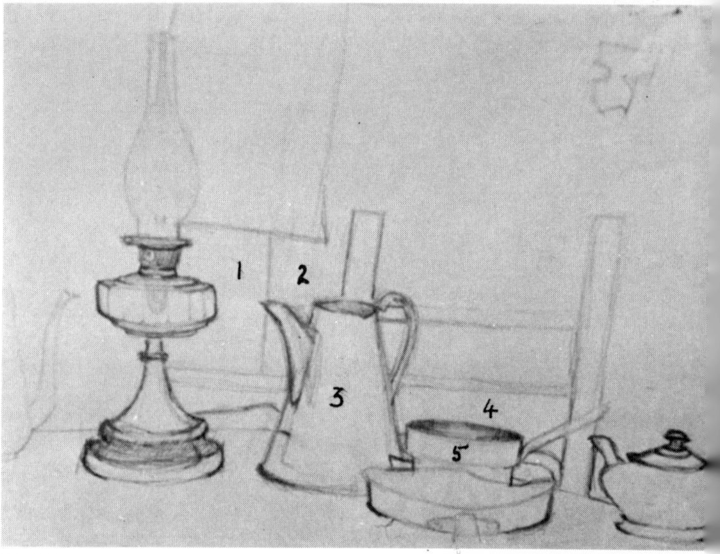

Fig 115

Fig 116

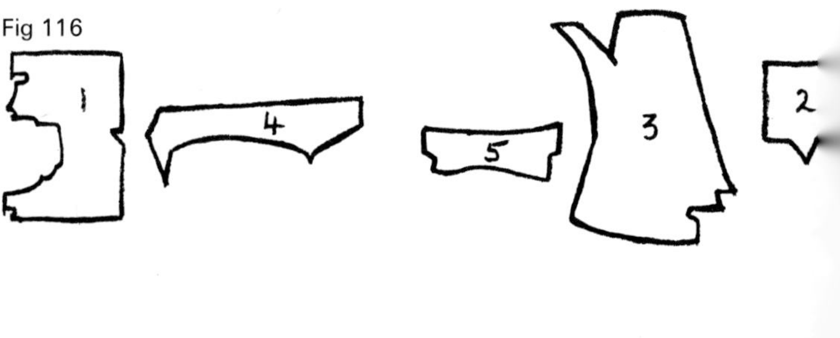

Figs 117–120 (*opposite*) Drawings showing good grasp of abstract shape, by students of varying age and ability

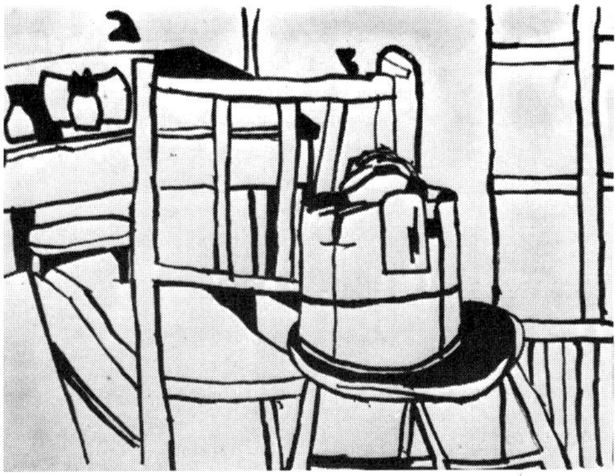

Fig 117

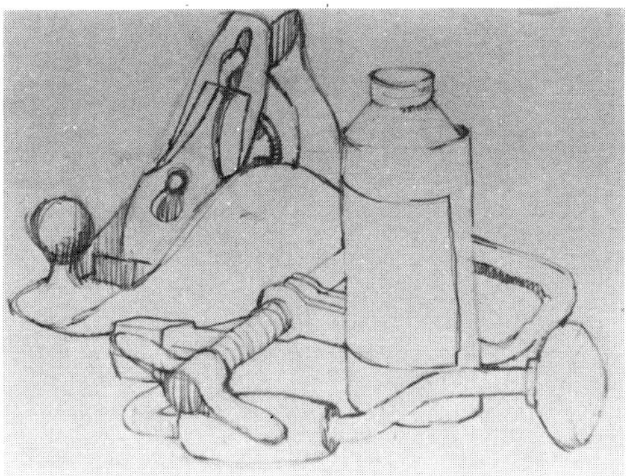

Fig 118

Fig 119

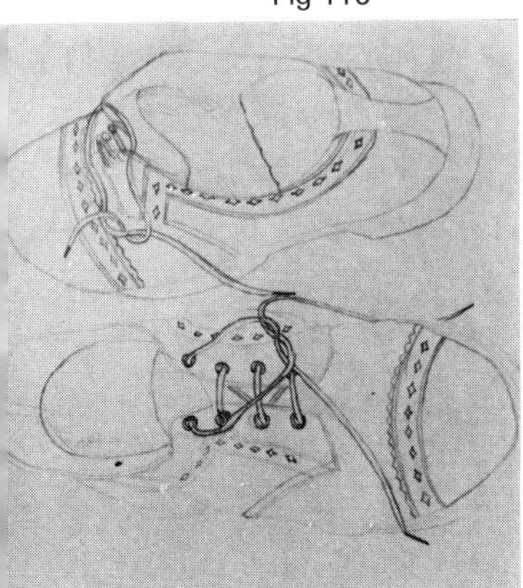

Fig 120

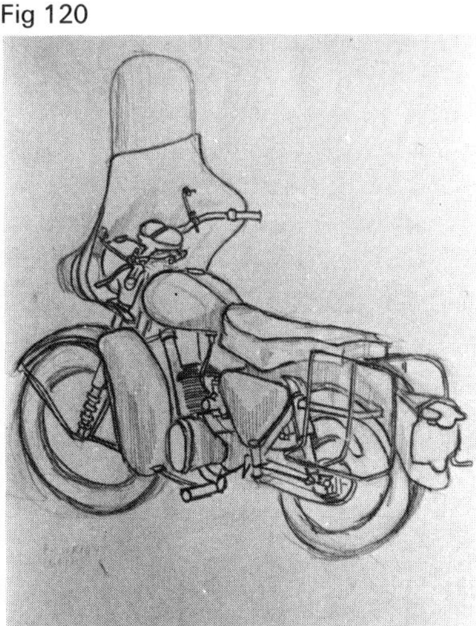

Can you find them?

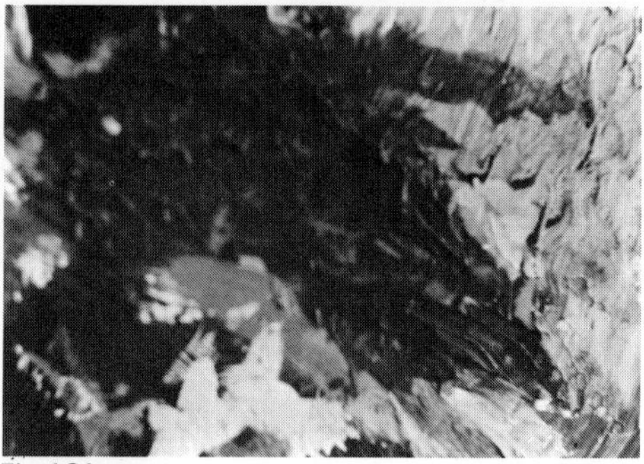

Fig 121

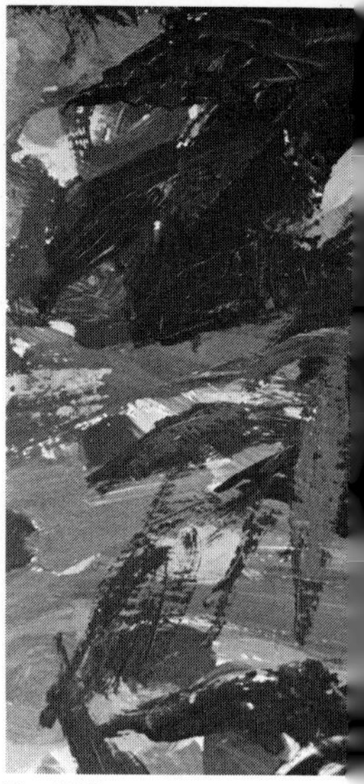

Fig 122

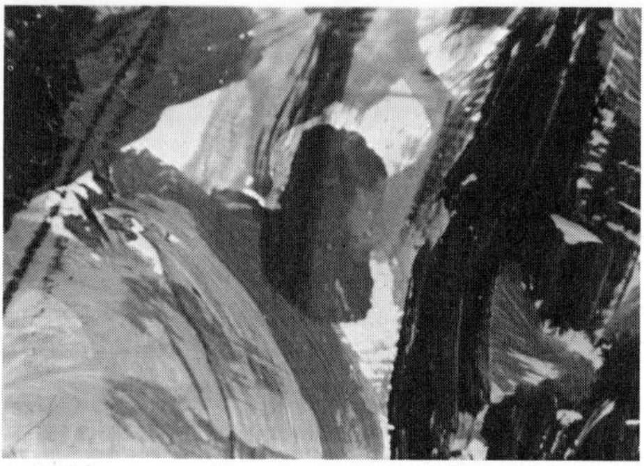

Fig 123

Fig 124

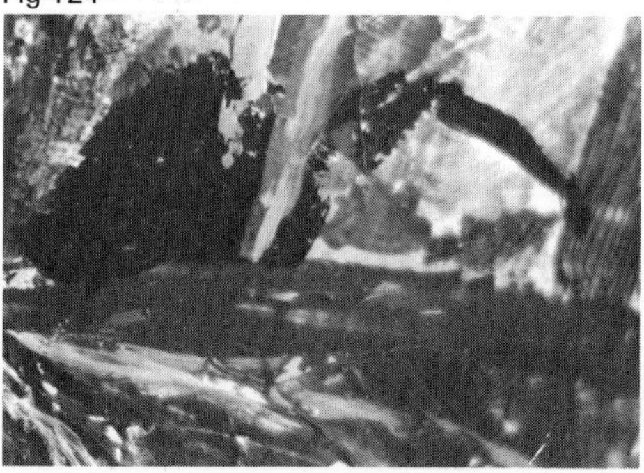

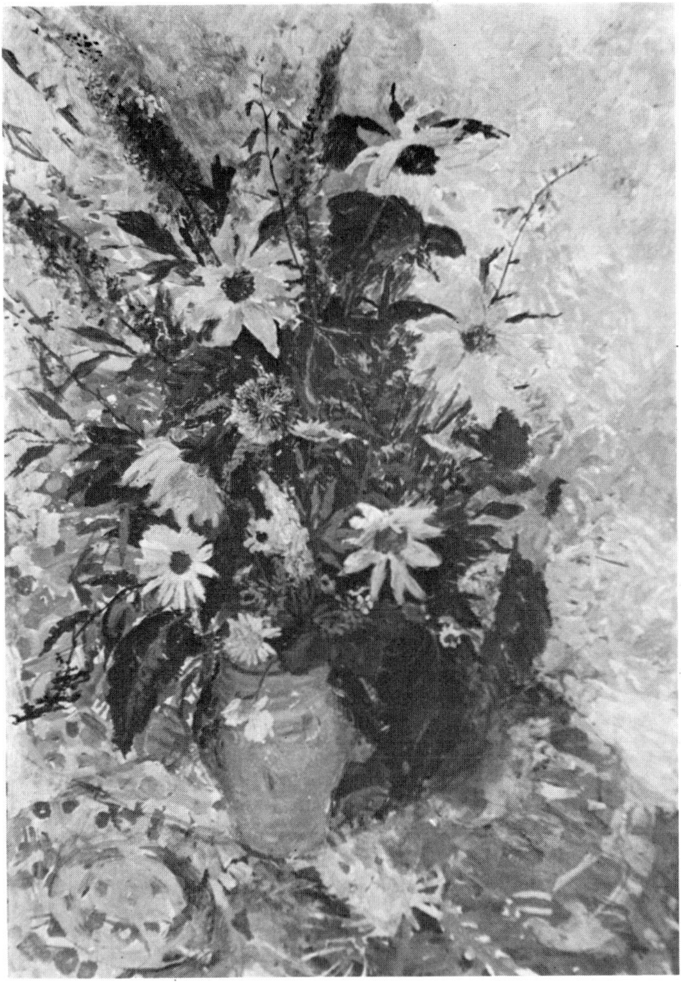

Fig 125

The four abstracts on page 82 are extracted by viewfinder from the above flower painting. They are not necessarily the same scale as the original. They *are* all printed the same way up. Can you find them? Their approximate locations are indicated on page 103.

Try the experiment of taking small pieces of one of your representational paintings and use these as motifs to make abstract designs, or to enlarge into paintings.

Application of squaring-up

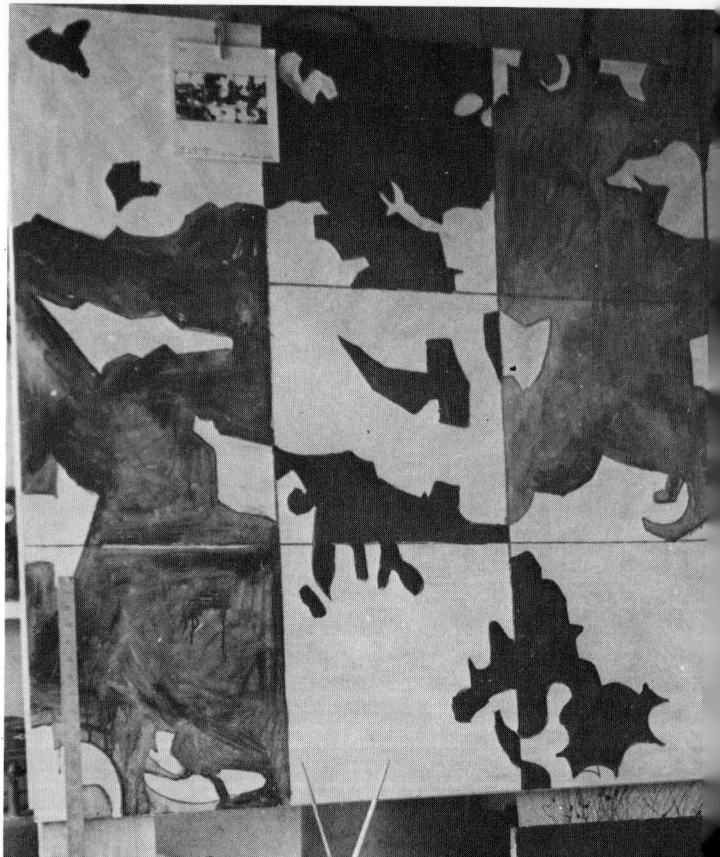

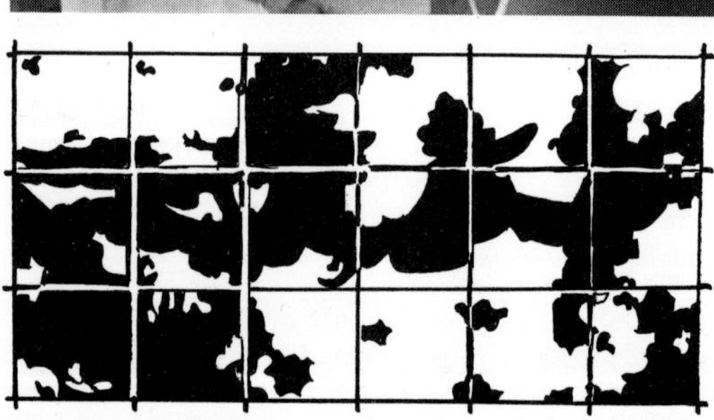

Fig 127

Fig 126

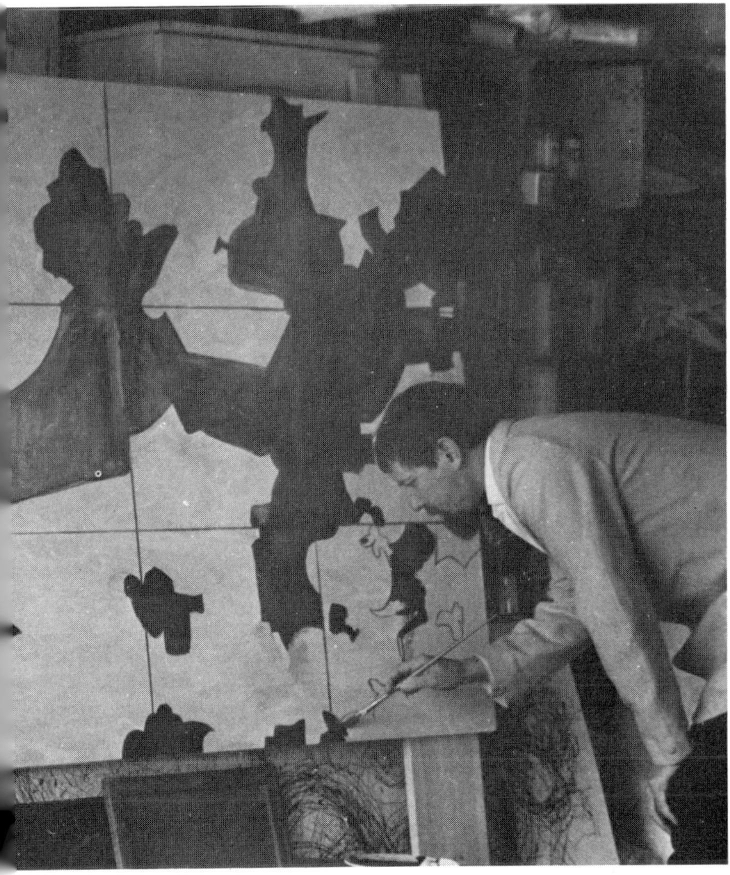

You will recognize the motif in fig. 127 opposite. You saw it first on page 55. You also saw the squaring-up method of enlarging on pages 56–7. Figs 126 and 127 on these two pages show an enlargement being carried out. Note the counterchange of the second from left vertical row of squares.

The finding of the motif, page 55, the principle of squaring-up, and the application of the principle of squaring-up are presented as three separate phases. Experience has convinced me that three modest bites makes for easy assimilation. Too big a mouthful all at once sometimes causes indigestion.

Points of view

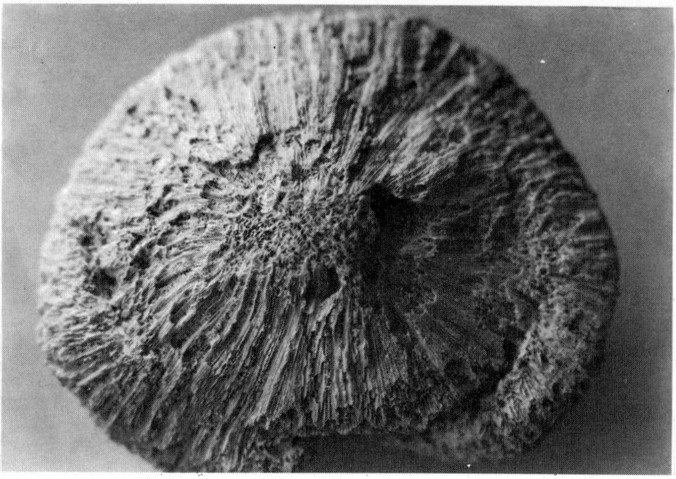

Fig 128

We have already considered the finding of abstract subject material by selection, by simplification, by section, by extraction, by accidental procedures, by progressive modification, by analysis, etc.

Another approach is to expose possible subject matter to varying treatments. Changing the position of the light, for instance, and, more important, looking from as many different points of view as possible. This has been hinted at already in the wall sequence on pages 25–7, though this example was of a variation on one sight-line only; in other words, from the same viewpoint each time but either nearer to, or farther away. Shift your position each time you look, or turn small objects round on all their axes, and the visual effect will vary accordingly. The illustrations which follow show a piece of coral. In fig. 128 it is viewed from below, in fig. 129 from the top, in fig. 130 from the side, in fig. 131 close to (full light), in fig. 133 close to (raking light from left). Figs 132 and 134 show two motifs taken from the coral.

If the abstract artist is sensitive to the subtlety and the uniqueness of forms, and he can make himself so, he will be able, by varying his viewpoint and also the light-source, to find many differing but related stimuli within one single form.

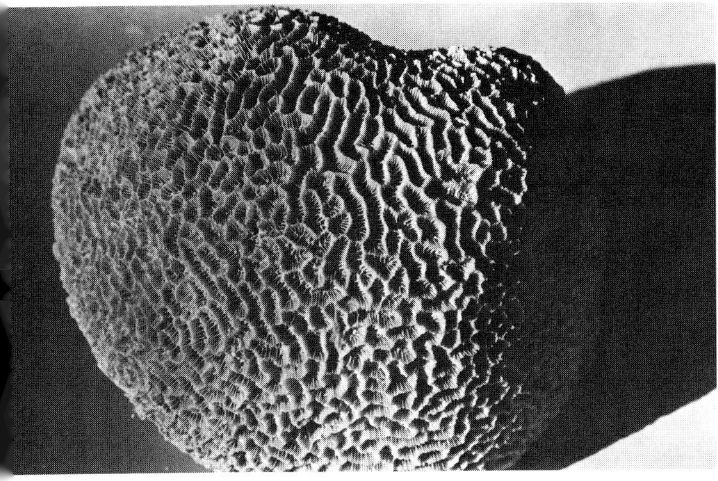

Fig 129

Fig 130

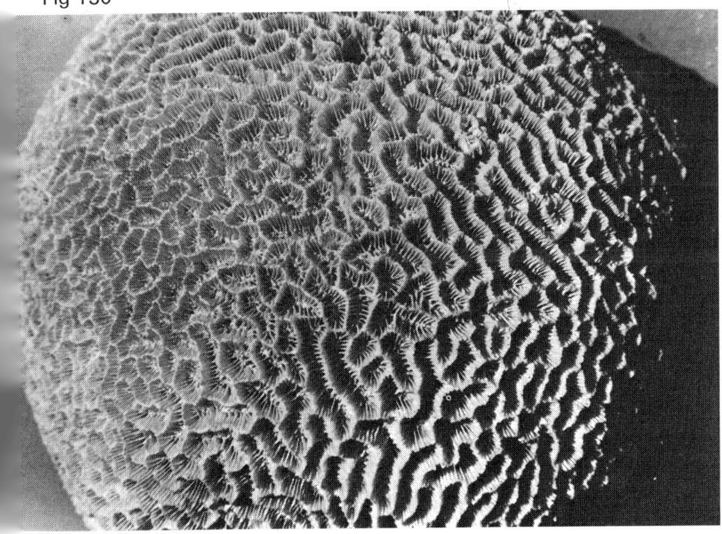

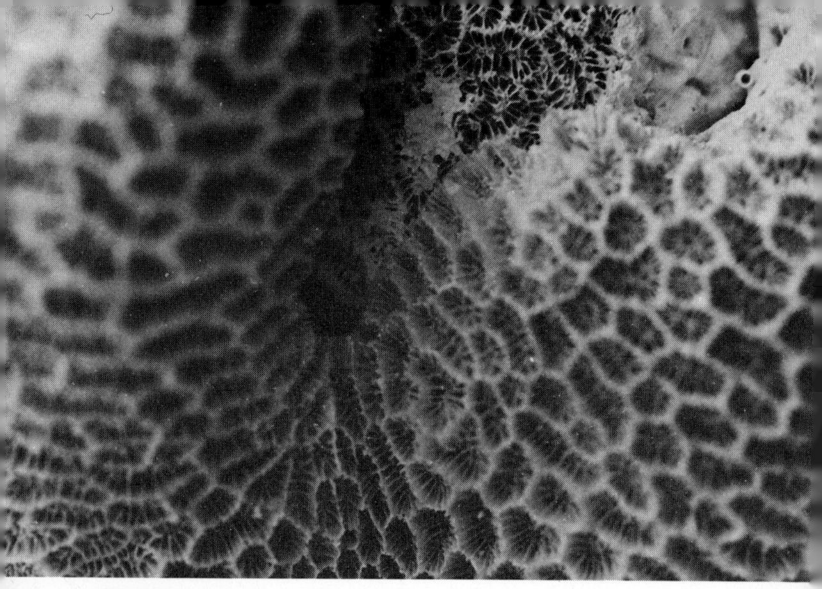

Fig 131

Fig 132

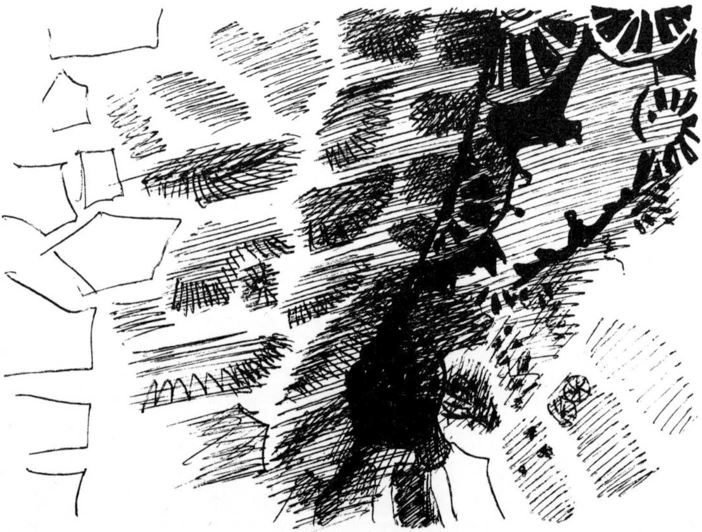

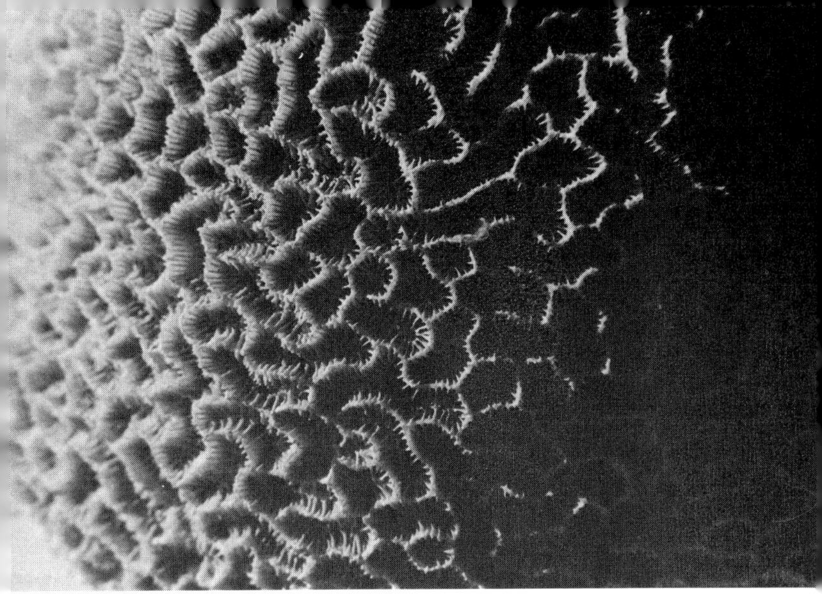

Fig 133

Fig 134

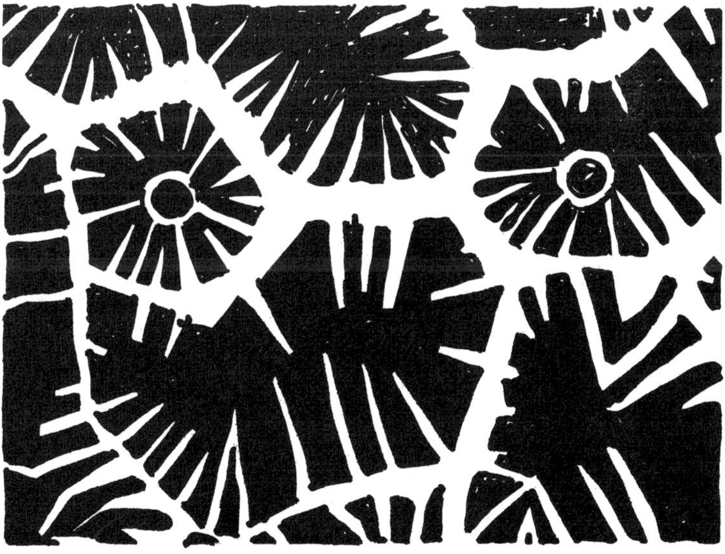

Ideograph, pictograph, symbol

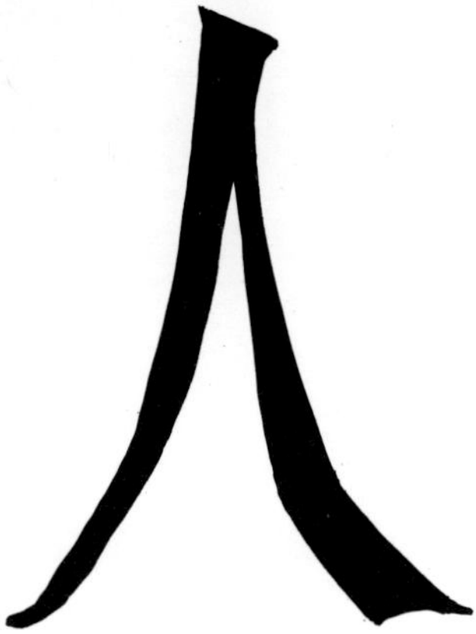

Fig 135

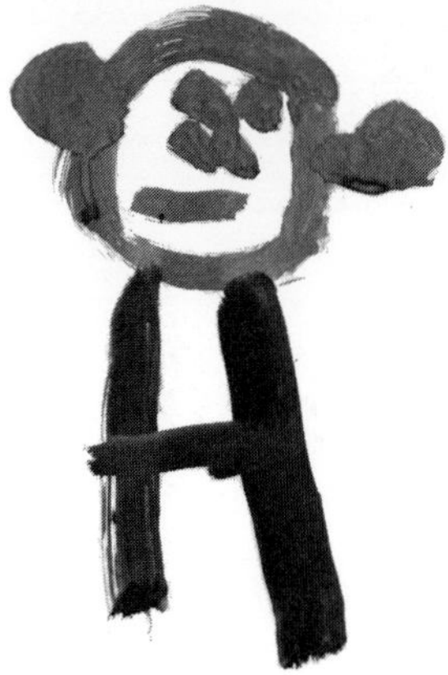

Fig 136

You will recall that on page 16 we discussed two commonly-accepted meanings of the term abstract, in art. One implies the use of abstract form, line, colour, etc., in a non-representational way, fig. 17. The other begins with representational forms and, by simplifying them, produces pictures which are more abstract than representational, fig. 13.

There is a third method of abstract expression which is less obvious and yet more universal than the other two. It is a method in which the artist invents his own personal pictograph language. He develops his own ideographs. He expresses his personal ideas by means of his own symbols.

Ancient forms of writing use pictographs based on abstracts of visual forms. The Chinese character for man is shown in fig. 135. Dr Bernhard Karlgren, in his book *The Chinese Language*, suggests this symbol was originally based on a man marching.

The very young child uses drawing as a means of communication. A typically childish symbol for a human being is shown in fig. 136.

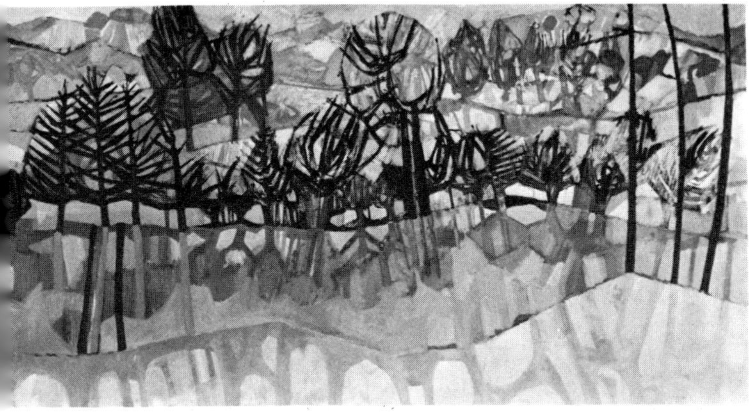

Fig 137

In our time in England L. S. Lowry has produced his own pictograph of the human form, which is not so far removed from the Chinese character.

All these symbols are non-realistic. The child, in particular, uses a symbol which is almost as remote from the recognizable image of the human form as is the Chinese character; but to the child it is real. What he wishes to communicate is real.

Egyptian, Gothic, Persian art have their own characteristic art symbols.

The two landscapes accompanying this section, figs 137 and 138, by a talented young woman painter, show how the artist analyzes the landscape, simplifies the main areas and translates, or paraphrases, the rest. She does not paint trees. She invents her own abstract symbols for trees. She builds up her picture with abstract forms which symbolize trees. In other words she paints an abstract analogy.

The image of the Virgin in the earliest Russian icons, and the Byzantine Madonnas in their golden backgrounds, employ

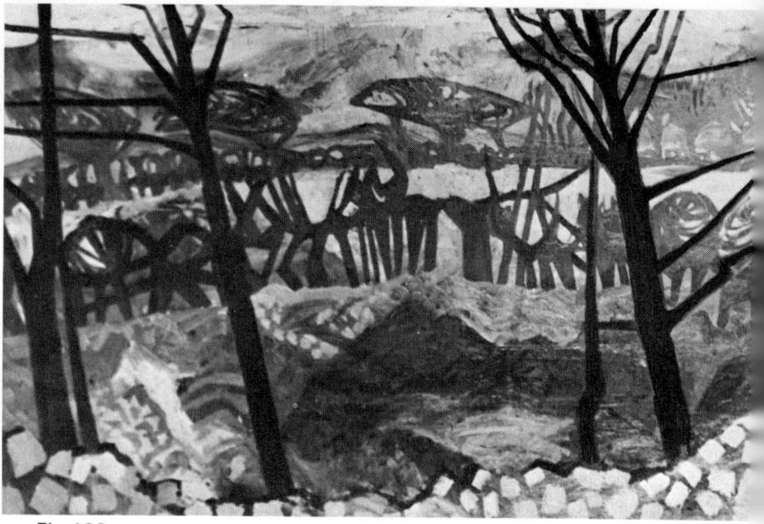

Fig 138

another kind of symbolism, at a different level, aiming at religious indoctrination. Realism is firmly rejected, and is replaced by the abstract of femininity.

Take your sketchbook. Seek out a series of characterful landscape images. Make drawings of them. Take them home and turn them into landscape symbols. Then try composing a picture using the symbols you have abstracted.

Abstract art and the community

The creative arts are the products of the philosophies and the social conditions of the civilizations in which they exist. They reflect the character of their times.

But the arts are not only a mirror to their times. On the other side of the coin, the forms evolved by the truly creative artist quickly affect our environment, and particularly the design of everyday commodities. The influence of Art Nouveau on the design of the Paris Metro station entrances and some of the architecture of that city at the turn of the century are persistent evidence of the fact.

The abstract artists have had a profound effect upon design in our day, especially upon industrial and domestic design. One influence they have had is the development in the public mind of a new awareness of qualities – the natural beauty of woods, of fibres, of glass, of plastics. They have awakened a new sense of the relationships of shapes one to another, and of the development of formal beauties arising out of processes, and of natural textures and colours as opposed to inappropriate applied decoration.

I would go so far as to say that Piet Mondrian, Ben Nicholson, Georges Braque and Picasso significantly influenced the appearance of my radio set, my refrigerator, the radiator in my house; the new railway terminal, the airport, Coventry Cathedral.

Abstract artists, at their level, and study of abstract art, at our level, strip away superficialities, and cause us to concentrate upon the inherent natural qualities of texture, form and colour. In doing this we find, anew, subtle qualities of beauty to enrich our lives.

Fig. 139 shows a central heating unit and fig. 140 a modern bank-front, both of which, it seems to me, have some kinship with Nicholson and Mondrian.

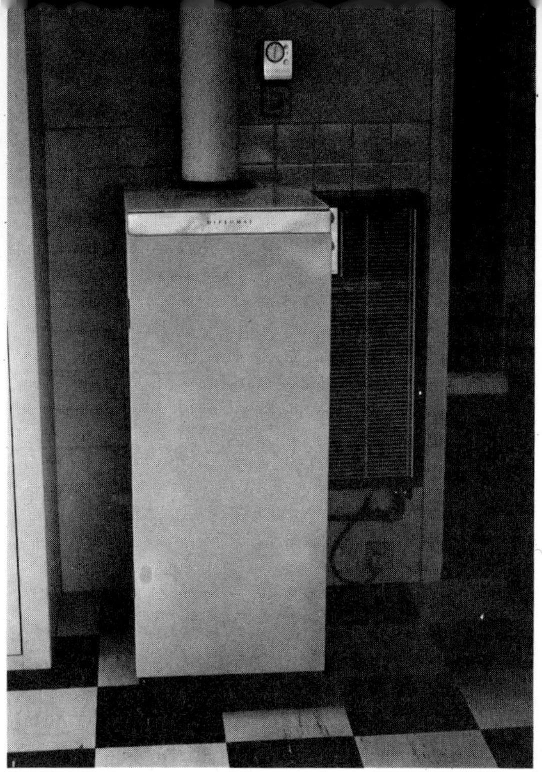

Fig 139

Fig 140

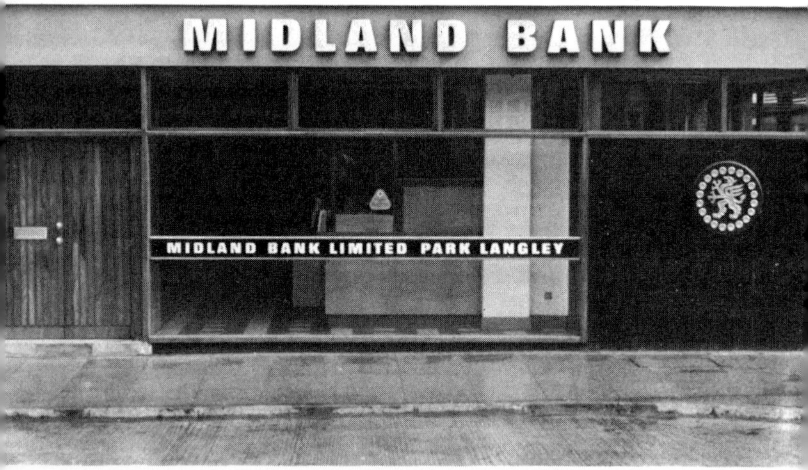

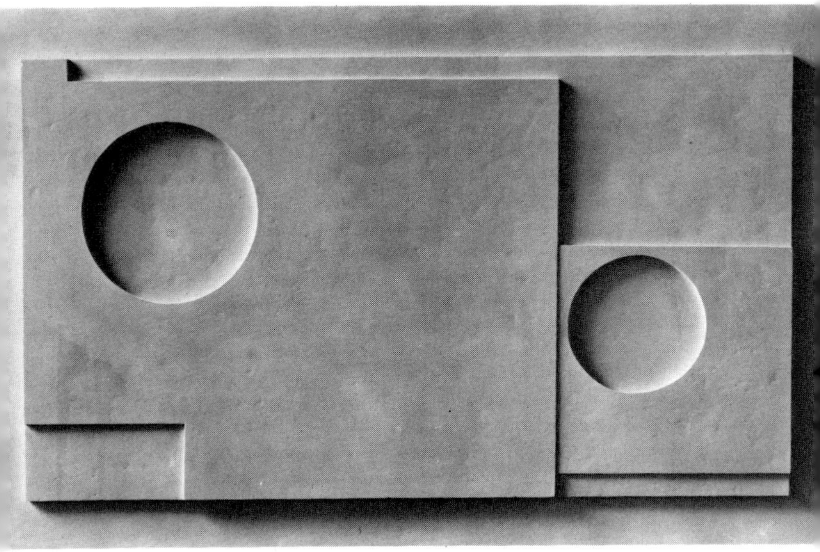

Fig 141 A typically austere design by Ben Nicholson, *White Relief*. Tate Gallery, London

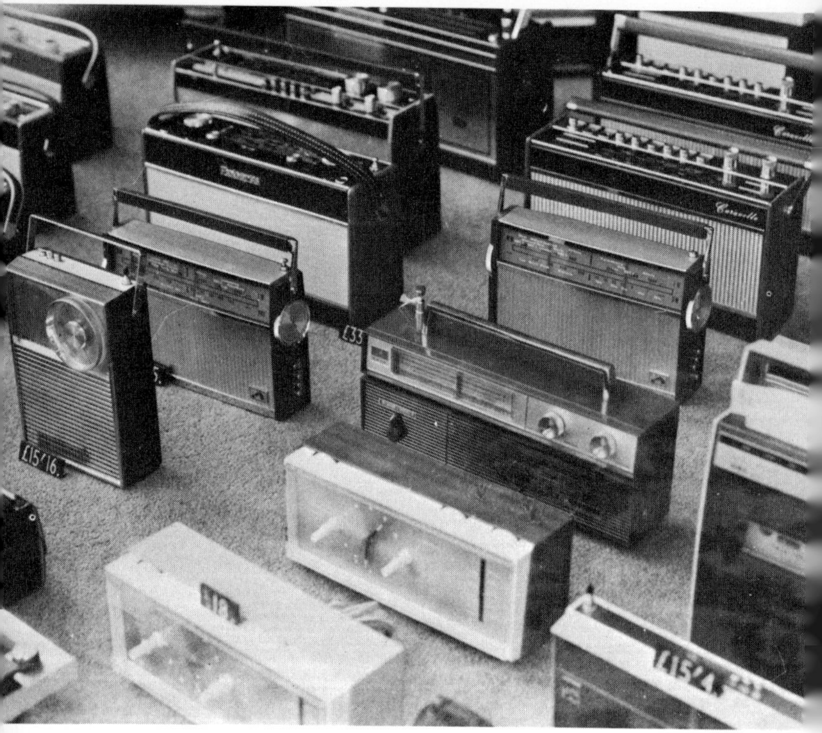

Fig 142 Look at the display of goods in the window of any electrical store and you will see the influence of contemporary art on the design of radio sets, electric fires etc.

Vision

The word 'vision' is a loaded term if ever there was one. It can mean anything, from an Old Testament prophet lying on a mound of stones with clouds of golden angels floating above his head, to the army recruit trying to read the medical officer's sight-test card. It can mean the young man's dream of a girl floating down the staircase into his arms, or William Blake's vision of the infinite.

The blind can see visions.

The so-called artist's vision has more than one component.

Looking is little more than the superficial taking-into-account of people, and of objects, to avoid bumping against them, tripping over them, or falling into them.

Seeing means much more. It implies becoming aware of an object, recognizing its existence and its meaning, assessing and appreciating its physical qualities, mentally registering its nature and so on.

Every sighted person looks. Not so many see. Looking and seeing are the two physical components of vision.

The other components are metaphysical. They include mental awareness, creative perception, imaginative conception, analytical appreciation.

The normal physical processes of looking and seeing act as 'starters' for a more complex and more comprehensive creative activity. Seeing is one of the programming processes of the artistic computer. What you look at, and what you see, starts your artist's mind working. The way the mind works, in response to what the eye sees, conditions what goes onto the paper or canvas, or stone or wood, or whatever is the medium of expression.

Above all else the artist must train himself not merely to look, but to see; and, having seen, to compute, to manipulate, to organize, to reconstruct, to translate, to transcribe and sometimes, but not often, to imitate.

The aim of this book is to help you to extend your vision, in all senses of the word.

That almost indefinable term 'the artist's vision' is made manifest by what the artist does with what he sees or what he imagines.

Colour

Colour is a powerful factor in our lives. Who would want to live in a room painted dark grey? Once you have decided the make and the model of your next motor car, the most important decision to be taken is, 'what colour?'. We refer to colour all the time— 'Green doesn't suit me. He was purple with rage. She was deathly white. In a brown study; blue with cold; green with envy. He's yellow!' It is the luminous *colours* of the sunset which root you to the spot. It was Gauguin who said 'six square feet of green is greener than six square inches'.

Colour influences our reactions, our environment, the choices we make. It has a dynamism and a decorative power of its own, irrespective of subject. It is a creator of atmosphere. Certain colours match certain emotional states. Colour can be used to generate specific emotional reactions; a good example of this is Picasso's use of colour during his Blue Period – blue was used in an emotive way to reinforce the atmosphere of poverty and depression which pervaded much of his work at that time. If you do not know these beautiful works you *must* study them in this context.

It is not possible to explain 'red' in words. It is not possible to experience red by reading about it. To understand and experience red you must be visually involved with red. It doesn't help, much, to know that red is a primary colour. The only way to really know colour is to experiment with colour. To explore personally all the pigments and methods of applying them you can find, to watch what happens as you experiment with mixings and different techniques of painting.

Some musicians have absolute pitch; they can name any note by hearing the sound only. You should train yourself to differentiate between varying degrees of colour, i.e. different intensities, different tones. The following exercises will help you:

1. Take a piece of white paper or cardboard 14 in.×12 in. Cut a rectangular hole in the centre 6 in.×4 in., and use this as a viewfinder. Take it out to the nearest tree with a thick enough trunk. Pin the paper to the trunk. Study the trunk through the rectangular hole. See how many different colours you can find in that 6 in.× 4 in. piece of trunk. Write down descriptions of the colours on the margins of the paper. Let your descriptions be as accurate as words will allow – 'speckled dull greenish yellow; medium grey with a touch of blueish mauve; ice-cream pink'. You will be surprised what a lot of colours you will find.

2. Set up a still-life subject in which every item is green, i.e. a green back-drop, a green ground to stand the subject on, a green

book, a green apple, a spray of green leaves, a green plate, a cucumber, a green bottle. Make a painting of it. You will be compelled to make nice visual judgements, and subtle adjustments in mixing the greens. Are you thinking 'this is not abstract'? The subject isn't, I agree, though you *could* abstract it, but the solving of the problem posed by the greens is the solving of an abstract problem.

Repeat this exercise with other groups – all whites, all blacks, reds only, blues, yellows, browns only, and so on.

3. Make five mixings of neutral greys of varying tones, in any medium of your choice, and set them out in a row as follows:

DARK GREY	MEDIUM DARK GREY	MEDIUM GREY	MEDIUM LIGHT GREY	LIGHT GREY

Now look around you, wherever you are at this moment. How many pure, spectrum, colours can you see? By spectrum colours I mean pure red, orange, yellow, green, blue, violet. My guess is you won't see many. For instance what is the colour of the nearest piece of wood furniture? Is it a pure colour? Probably not. The chair I am sitting in as I write this is made of teak. It is not a pure colour, it is a medium-tone rusty brown. The nearest pure colour to it is orange, but the chair is much greyer in quality than pure orange. Which of the above five greys is nearest in tone to the tone of the chair colour? The medium grey. So I mix medium neutral grey and orange, and I get a fair approximation of teak colour, a good colour-match. Navy blue is dark grey plus prussian blue. My garden wall is medium light grey plus yellow ochre. The Siamese cat is medium grey plus a very little ultramarine. Make half-a-dozen colour-matchings a day by this method, and see how, in as short a time as a week, it will quicken your colour responses.

4. Let us remind ourselves again of the colour sequence of the spectrum – red, orange, yellow, green, blue, violet. Take, say, a simple landscape subject and, as you paint it, experiment by transposing each one of its constituent colours by one tone – so that all the reds in the subject are painted as orange, all the oranges are shown as yellows, all the yellows are made green, all the greens are translated into blues and all the blues are rendered as violets. This is the same sort of process as that employed by the musician who transposes his music from D major to E major. The change in tonality produces a positive and yet abstract effect, often very stimulating.

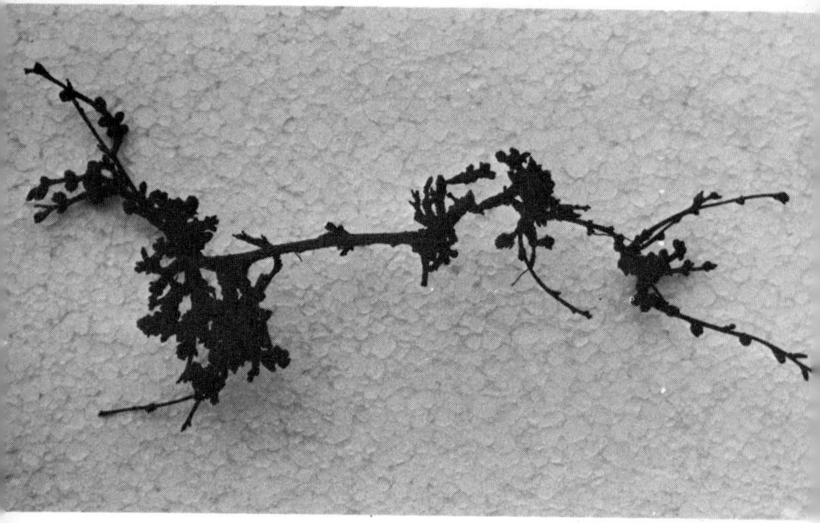

Fig 143 Photograph of the silver birch twig from which the frontispiece drawing was made

The analogy with music is a valid one. Harmonious sound and harmonious colour are exact equivalents in the two media.
This is as far as we can go about colour within the format of this book.

To me colour is the most significant aspect of painting. You may not agree but, if you do, and if you would like to take the subject further, you would find *Colour for the Artist* by Hans Schwarz, in the same series as this book, very helpful.

Conclusion

I am aware there are gaps in this book. Nothing is included about, for instance, the abstract forms of Kinetic Art, or about Op Art. You will notice other omissions. It is not a 'how-to-do-it' in the usual sense. It does not tell you how to paint an abstract picture. It does attempt to explain what abstract art is, to draw a distinction between an abstract painting and an abstract method of painting.

It positively attempts to persuade you there is a bottomless reservoir of subject material, for painting and creative expression generally, ready to be tapped if certain techniques of visual exploration are used. The few I have described will, I hope, suggest other lines of enquiry to you.

Be inquisitive. Be prepared to forsake the conventional concept of the artist's subject matter – still life, portrait, landscape.

Many non-professionals, who are just beginning to practise painting, mistakenly think that the production of traditional pictures is the only worthwhile aim of the painter; and because the painting of such pictures requires a good deal of practice, determination and patience, many aspirants, even some with good natural ability, become discouraged and finally give up.

This is a sad waste of the creative energy which persists, to a greater or lesser degree, in all of us. Some of the techniques outlined in this book, on the other hand (and this is not an attempt to make the case for taking short cuts and the easy way out), suggest channels of expression well within everybody's capabilities which provide aesthetic satisfaction. They call for some manual dexterity, but much more for a sense of harmony, balance, colour, texture, form, shape, tone.

Develop your sensitivity to abstract values, and you will acquire the ability to make your own personal statements about those aspects of your environment which interest you. In doing so you will produce works of art, and they will have the same magic and significance as the pebble on the beach, because they will share those same visual and formal qualities which are fundamentals of the physical structure of the world in which we live.

Further reading

Abstract Painting and Sculpture in America by Richie; Museum of Modern Art, New York 1951

Art Now by Herbert Read; Faber, London 1933; Pitman, New York 1960

Basic Design; the Dynamics of Visual Form by Maurice de Sausmarez; Studio Vista, London 1964; Reinhold, New York 1964

Colour for the Artist by Hans Schwarz; Studio Vista, London 1968; Watson-Guptill, New York 1968

Despite Straight Lines by Joseph Albers and Francois Bucher; Yale University Press, New York 1962

Dictionary of Modern Painting; Methuen, London 1956

Education of Vision by Gyorgy Kepes; Studio Vista, London 1965; Braziller, New York 1965

Introduction to the Visual Arts (symposium); Harrap, London 1968; Tudor, New York 1968

Kaleidoscope of Modern Art by Neville Weston; Harrap, London 1968; Verry, Connecticut 1968

Observer's Book of Modern Art by William Gaunt; Warne, London and New York 1964

On Modern Art by Paul Klee; Faber, London 1966; Dutton, New York 1967

Structure in Art and Science by Gyorgy Kepes; Studio Vista, London 1965; Braziller, New York 1965

Textures by Phil Brodatz; Dover, New York 1966

The Art of Colour by Johannes Itten; Reinhold, New York 1961

The Collections of the Tate Gallery; Tate Gallery, London 1967

The Meaning of Art by Herbert Read; Faber, London 1931; Penguin, Maryland 1959

The Nature and Art of Motion by Gyorgy Kepes; Studio Vista, London 1965; Braziller, New York 1965

The Thinking Eye (the teaching notes of Paul Klee); Lund Humphries, London 1961; Wittenborn, New York 1964

Solutions

Page 10
Fig. 4 rock strata. Fig. 5 detail of a representational flower-painting. Fig. 6 hoarding, Dijon. Fig. 7 *Boon*, detail, painting by James Brookes. Tate Gallery, London. Fig. 8 *Ochre Painting*, detail, by William Scott. Tate Gallery, London. Fig. 9 wall in Durham

Page 23
Fig. 25 *Rhythm and Harmony*. 4 followed up by 1.
Fig. 26 *Balance.* Off-balance – 2 and 3. Unimaginatively balanced – 4 and 5. Varied and satisfying balance – 1 and 6

Page 36
The Greek island of Mikanos, seen from the air

Page 43 A rose hip

Page 48 Textures
Middle row (left to right), nettle stems, reeds, string
Bottom row (left to right), split sunflower stems with pith, dried montbretia leaves, rolled newspapers

Page 68
Fig. 96 *Two Figures (Menhirs)* by Barbara Hepworth. Tate Gallery, London
Fig. 97 Sea-worn pebble

Page 83
Can You Find Them? Consider the bouquet of flowers to be a clock face.
Look for fig. 121 at 4.0 o'clock, fig. 122 at 9.0, fig. 123 at 7.0, fig. 124 at just turned 12.0

Index

Absolute pitch 98
Abstract analogy 91
Abstract Expressionists 60
Abstract qualities 9
Accidental effect 61
Action Painters 60
Aerosol 49, 61
Art Nouveau 93
Artistic computer 97

Background shapes 46
Balance 23
Bayeux tapestry 79
Blue Period, Picasso 98
Braque, Georges 60, 93
Byzantine Madonna 91

Camera 63
Cézanne 44
Child art 16
Clay 47
Collage 45
Colour 19, 98
Colour match 99
Counterchange 73
Coventry Cathedral 93
Crayon, grease 55

Decorators' lining paper 56
Domestic design 93
Doodle 59
Drawing 79

Embroidery 36
Environment 24, 39, 41, 51, 63, 93, 101

Finding 67
Form 20
Found abstract 67

Gauguin 98
Generating process 59
Gothic manuscripts 79
Grass stems 49

Harmony 22, 46
Hepworth, Barbara 103
Hilton, R. 13
Hitchens, Ivon 13

Ideograph 90
Industrial design 93

Karlgren, Dr Bernhard 90

Line 22
Lowry, L. S. 91

Microscope 63
Mikanos 103
Mondrian, Piet 93
Moore, Henry 8
Motif 44

Nash, John 12
Nash, Paul 12
Nicholson, Ben 93, 95

Optical aids 63

Palette knife 60
Pattern 20, 75
Picasso 7, 8, 93, 98
Pictograph 90
Playing card 75
Points of view 86
Pollock, Jackson 61, 62
Printing 54
Projecting 52

Red cabbage 41
Rhythm 22
Royal Academy 16
Rubbings 55
Russian icons 91

Screen 27
Screenprint 43
Sections 40, 41
Seeing 97
Sensitivity 8
Shape 20
Simplification 76
Sketchbook 63, 79
Spectrum colour 99
Squaring-up 56, 85
Sunflowers 36
Symbol 90, 91

Texture 21
Tonal change 99
Tone 19
Trigger-mechanisms 44
Turner, J. M. W. 12, 14

Viewfinder 39, 54, 83, 98
Vision 97
Visual exploration 51

Water pistol 61